THE PENNINE WAY
NATIONAL TRAIL

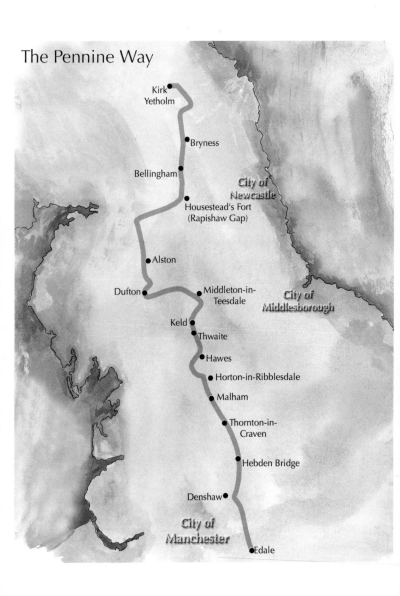

The Pennine Way

Kirk
Yetholm

Bryness

Bellingham

City of
Newcastle

Housestead's Fort
(Rapishaw Gap)

Alston

Dufton

Middleton-in-
Teesdale

City of
Middlesborough

Keld

Thwaite

Hawes

Horton-in-Ribblesdale

Malham

Thornton-in-
Craven

Hebden Bridge

Denshaw

City of
Manchester

Edale

THE PENNINE WAY NATIONAL TRAIL
THE ALL-IN-ONE PRACTICAL GUIDE FOR WALKERS

by
Martin Collins

2 POLICE SQUARE, MILNTHORPE, CUMBRIA LA7 7PY
www.cicerone.co.uk

© M. Collins 1998, 2003
2nd edition 2003
ISBN 1 85284 386 1
A catalogue record for this book is available from the British Library.
Photographs by the author unless stated.

For Paul, Rosie and Sarah
That they too may one day find happiness tramping the Pennines

About the Author

Martin Collins is a freelance author, photo-journalist and cartographer, as well as a contributor to the UK outdoor media. He has written over twenty books for walkers embracing the coast, mountains and countryside of the UK and parts of Europe. He has three children, and lives in North Wales on the edge of the Snowdonia National Park.

Other Cicerone guidebooks by Martin Collins
Treks in the Dolomites (with Gillian Price)
Chamonix – Mont Blanc
North York Moors
The Teesdale Way
South West Way
A Walker's Guide to the Isle of Wight (with Norman Birch)

Front cover: High Cup on the fells above Dufton

CONTENTS

The Pennine Way

Route Description

Appendices

ACKNOWLEDGEMENTS

Grateful thanks to Steve Westwood of the Countryside Agency for coordinating the updating of this edition and providing other helpful data.

All cartoons, maps and photographs are by the author unless otherwise specified.

This book has been compiled in accordance with the *Guidelines for Writers of Path Guides* produced by the Outdoor Writers' Guild

Please visit: **NationalTrail.co.uk**

Advice to Readers

Readers are advised that while every effort is taken by the author to ensure the accuracy of this guidebook, changes can occur which may affect the contents. It is advisable to check locally on transport, accommodation, shops, etc, but even rights of way can be altered.

The publisher would welcome notes of any such changes.

THE PENNINE WAY

The Pennine Way begins, wholly appropriately, in the centre of England, historically the heartland of the country's outdoor movement. Ringed by motorways and the industrial conurbations of Sheffield, Derby, The Potteries, Manchester and Huddersfield, the 542 square miles (140,000 hectares) of the Peak District National Park contains some of the wildest and loveliest countryside in Britain. Each year some 20 million day visitors flock here yet paradoxically the general public has not always been welcome.

Following World War I, and especially during the Depression years, these moors and dales represented a release from the grime and drudgery of city life. At weekends, thousands poured out by train to relish a few precious hours of freedom and fresh air in the hills. Wide horizons, the challenge of physical exertion, walking alone or in friendly company come rain or shine, all helped to counterbalance lives otherwise blighted by squalor and long working hours.

In 1926 John Derry, that standard-bearer of the early rambling movement, summed up the mood of the time in his guidebook *Across the Derbyshire Moors*: 'And yet it does one good to get into this upland, age-long solitude, where the primeval world is felt to be a mighty fact, linked on to us.'

However, there were considerable obstacles facing walkers in those pre-National Park days. Land was mainly in private ownership (as it still is) and to protect their incomes obtained from grouse-shooting, landowners barred ramblers from vast tracts of Kinder Scout, Bleaklow and the eastern moors. 'Trespassers will be prosecuted' signs were erected and immediately dubbed 'wooden liars' because trespass, of course, is not a prosecutable offence. More seriously, armed gamekeepers were posted at strategic access points.

Understandably, resentment flared up when ramblers were thwarted while asserting their 'right to roam'. Ugly scenes erupted and rewards were offered in local newspapers for anyone who could identify photographed trespassers. The more militant ramblers regularly risked spells in prison for their passionately held beliefs. But as John Derry observed: 'Nothing keeps alive the spirit of revolt and iconoclasm so fiercely as a refusal to the general community of the use of their eyes over beautiful remote tracts of the earth, under the plea of private ownership.'

Fired by unemployment and growing political awareness among working class people during the 1920s and early 1930s, the access movement gained momentum. Protest rallies were held near Castleton

Pennine wayfarers on the route between Edale and Jacob's Ladder, Stage 1
(Photograph by Paddy Dillon)

expressing a common desire for free access to crags and moorland: it is a call whose message remains alive to this day.

Everything came to a head with the famous Mass Trespass of 24th April 1932. Their sights sets firmly on reaching the forbidden Kinder Scout plateau, some 400 ramblers set off from Hayfield. Because the event had been widely publicised, they were met at Sandy Heys just below the plateau edge by groups of keepers. With emotions running high, verbal exchanges escalated to physical scuffles, as a result of which six ramblers received gaol sentences of between two and six months for assault and riotous assembly.

Few access concessions were granted for a number of years but such sustained public defiance against the landowning aristocracy did eventually create a steady shift towards the view that the countryside should be there for everyone to enjoy. By 1949 this concept had become enshrined in the National Parks and Access to the Countryside Act. Two years later, in April 1951, the Peak District was established as Britain's first National Park and in 1965 the Pennine Way became Britain's first official long-distance trail.

In fact the idea of a continuous footpath from Derbyshire's Peak District to the Scottish Borders had first been mooted back in 1935 by Tom Stephenson in a newspaper article, but in those days there was no helpful legislation, no chance of concessions from the water authorities and grouse shooting fraternity. However, already the rambling clubs and the newly formed Youth Hostels Association had begun to open up the

Baldersdale is a broad, quiet dale surrounded by extensive moorlands, Stage 9 (Photograph by Paddy Dillon)

Walkers perched on the limestone pavement high above Malham Cove on Stage 7 (Photograph by Paddy Dillon)

countryside to walkers over most of England and Wales (Kinder Scout and Bleaklow excepted!). Tom Stephenson's proposal met with enthusiastic support and in February 1938 representatives of open-air organisations held a conference at Hope in Derbyshire and inaugurated the Pennine Way Association. What the conference agreed encapsulates the very essence of the Pennine Way:

'The wide, health-giving moorlands and high places of solitude, the features of natural beauty and the places of historical interest along the Pennine Way give this route a special character and attractiveness which should be available for all time as a natural heritage of the youth of the country and of all who feel the call of the hills and lonely places.'

Having devised a route for the Pennine Way utilising existing footpaths, old miners' and drovers' tracks, Roman roads and green lanes, it was concluded that although about 180 miles (290km) of public rights-of-way could be used, some 70 miles (113km) of new paths were required.

The National Parks Commission adopted the proposed line of the Pennine Way with a few minor changes and in their second report stated that:

'The Pennine Way will be a strenuous high-level route through predominantly wild country and is intended for walkers of some experience. It will involve a fair element of physical exertion and a willingness to endure rough going. While the greater part of the Way is across existing well-trodden tracks, the route in places crosses expanses of wild moorland devoid of prominent landmarks and consisting largely of peat, heather, bog and tussocks of rough grass. These sections of the route can be traversed only by strong walkers, and in bad weather they can be safely negotiated only by people who can steer a course by map and compass.'

From July 1951 onwards, local authorities worked on creating the necessary new rights-of-way and on 24th April 1965, at a mass gathering on Malham Moor, the then Minister of Land and Natural Resources, along with Tom Stephenson, Secretary of the Ramblers Association, declared the Pennine Way open and completed.

TERRAIN AND WEATHER

The ancient mountain forms and rock strata of England's spine were, in recent geological times, eroded away to a considerable extent by Ice Age glaciers: they smoothed the hillsides, broadened and scoured the valleys, and when they finally retreated they left behind moraines and layers of boulders and clay.

In broad terms the Pennines as we know them comprise three distinct regions: the peat moorlands from Derbyshire to the Aire Gap; the central moors from the Aire Gap to Stainmore; and the High Pennines between Stainmore and the River Tyne. (The Cheviots do not belong to the Pennines at all but were included in the Pennine Way as a means of extending the route to the Scottish Borders over challenging and unspoilt terrain.)

Unlike well defined mountains such as are found in the Lake District and Snowdonia, Pennine summits rarely distinguish themselves in a

Cam High-road above Cam Houses is based on an old Roman road on Stage 7 (Photograph by Paddy Dillon)

Easter dawn on Millstone Edge, Stage 3

clear-cut fashion. The higher tops may have specific names – Kinder Scout, Great Shunner Fell, Cross Fell – but (with a few exceptions such as Pen-y-ghent) they are more the culmination of swelling moorland surrounded by rolling ridges or plateaux than individual peaks.

Over the decades of its existence, the Pennine Way has become almost synonymous with hard going through endless bogs. Apart from intermittent relief in Malham's limestone country, in Upper Teesdale and along the other river valleys, much of the Way is, indeed, squelchy underfoot except in the driest conditions.

Peat is usually the culprit. These hills once supported woodlands of elm, oak and lime; it was tree clearance by Neolithic man, the first farmers, that began the long process of decline in tree cover. Eventually,

exposed to the elements, the land lay waste, its vegetation rotting down to form a thick peat layer. Resting on impervious Millstone Grit, the ground became waterlogged, producing the bogs so characteristic of the Dark Peak and the Cheviot Hills.

In the 17th-century Daniel Defoe had declared the Peak '...the most desolate, wild and abandoned country in England...' Even in our own times, that doyen of hillwalkers, Alfred Wainwright, described Bleaklow as '...an inhospitable wilderness of peat bogs over which progress on foot is very arduous...'. Happily the Pennines are not universally as bleak as their reputation, although there are admittedly some grim stretches! In recent years the Pennine Way Coordination Project has overseen the installation of flagpaths, emulating the old stone 'causeys', along which packhorse

The towering and menacingly overhanging limestone crags at Gordale Scar, near Malham (Stage 6 and 7) offers respite from the peat bogs encountered elsewhere (Photograph by Paddy Dillon)

Erosion control around Pen-y-Ghent has resulted in boardwalks being installed, Stage 6 (Photograph by Paddy Dillon)

trains once travelled over the moors carrying panniers laden with raw materials and commodities. The modern technique involves airlifting in flagstones reclaimed from old mill floors and other industrial demolition sites. Some of the worst sections of bogginess on the Pennine Way have thus been 'tamed'. The flagpaths are not to everyone's liking, removing the challenge, some say, from negotiating difficult terrain and navigating in mist. But as a long term anti-erosion measure these new path constructions are welcomed by the majority of walkers.

Perhaps, as Thomas Hardy said of Egdon Heath, such country '...appeals to a subtler and scarcer instinct, to a more recently learned emotion than that which responds to a sort of beauty called charming and fair...'.

Certainly countless ramblers have acquired a taste for the rougher, more sombre Pennine uplands which don't conform to our traditional aesthetic of landscape attractiveness.

Probably the most enduring of all Pennine Way images are those vast horizons, soundless except for running water, the rush of wind in heather and grasses, and the haunting cry of the curlew. Yet the archetypal Pennine moors are only half the picture. In between are descents into pastoral valleys and mill towns; encounters with the great reservoirs that quench the thirst of neighbouring conurbations; tranquil riverside paths; long ambling miles on old drovers' roads; thrilling interludes in the limestone scenery of the North Craven Fault and the Whin Sill formations of Upper Teesdale; Hadrian's Wall; forest rides; and the fascinating miscellany of lowland and hill farms whose influence on the landscape seems so mundane yet is so profound.

British weather is notoriously fickle and there may be longer term climate changes taking place due to global warming. On a trek the length of the Pennine Way you should go prepared for all kinds of weather conditions. It is worth remembering that for every 1000ft (300m) of height gained above sea level, the air temperature will be around three degrees Celsius lower. This means that for long stretches of trail the temperature will be some five degrees Celsius colder than in adjacent lowlands. In addition, winds blow more strongly over high ground as the prevailing airstream rises and accelerates to cross it. This process often produces cloud shrouding the tops in mist and also increases the amount of precipitation falling as rain or snow. So while a walk in the dales or forest may be quite tolerable during stormy weather, traversing the tops can turn into a tough battle against the elements, even in summer.

Conversely, prolonged dry weather – not unknown in recent years – creates problems of a different kind, especially during the summer months. Walking in heat can cause excessive fluid loss through sweating and there is added danger from the sun's harmful UV rays. Although at such times the bogs will have largely dried out, making the going easier, finding water to drink is much harder.

Conventionally the Pennine Way is walked south-to-north so that wind, weather and sun are more likely to be at your back for most of the route.

EQUIPMENT AND SAFETY

Experienced walkers will have their own tried-and-tested outdoor gear and will readily be able to assess what is needed for a trek on the Pennine Way. Those newer to walking (and long-distance walking in particular) may find the following notes useful.

Firstly, well fitting, comfortable boots add immeasurably to the enjoyment of walking. Put another way, ill fitting or inappropriate footwear can turn what should be an essentially pleasurable experience into sheer purgatory! Blisters and other injuries cannot be relied upon to simply clear up as the trek progresses – there is every likelihood they will get worse, especially when carrying a rucksack that is of necessity heavier than a

The Lakeland fells can be seen in the distance from Cross Fell summit along the route

normal daypack. More walkers abandon the Pennine Way from foot and knee problems than for any other reason. The best advice is to thoroughly try out new boots before attempting a long-distance walk, and similarly to test your existing pair over a couple of long days with a loaded rucksack.

Lightweight boots will be perfectly suitable, even trainers for some stretches and for use in settled weather. However, boots do need to be moderately waterproof which tends to rule out fabric designs with multiple seams. Gaiters or 'puttees' are invaluable for keeping socks dry and for preventing mud and water from entering the top of the boot.

What to wear depends to a large extent on the time of year, though as a general rule several thin layers of clothing are more versatile than one thick one. Garments manufactured from modern synthetic fibres provide excellent insulation as well as wicking perspiration away from your skin – infinitely preferable to the cold clamminess of wet cotton! For the same reason jeans are best avoided, being constricting and cold when damp and slow to dry out.

Shell clothing – cagoule and overtrousers – are virtually indispensable for protection against rain and wind, a dangerous combination even in summer. The more expensive 'breathable' garments will double as windproofs without the annoying condensation problems of cheaper PVC coated nylon. Whatever you wear, it is better to be 'wet and warm' than 'wet

and cold'. A woolly hat or cap can be worth its weight in gold: keep your head warm and the rest of you is unlikely to feel chilled.

Winter expeditions on the higher stretches of the Pennine Way should always be treated seriously. Clothing, equipment, and the walker wearing them should all be able to withstand potentially hostile weather. Winter extras might include warm headgear, gloves, emergency rations such as chocolate or mintcake, adequate drinks, a torch and whistle, a plastic survival bag (or tent) and spare warm clothing. Winter or summer, carry a small first aid kit and, of course, map and compass. In hot summer sunshine cover up with lightweight, loose-fitting clothes and a brimmed sunhat and remember to carry plenty of liquid. A high-factor suncream will protect exposed skin against the harmful effects of ultra-violet radiation. At such times of the year special care is needed to avoid starting a moorland or forest fire. Insect repellent can be a godsend during the midge-biting season when the wee beasties are capable of making life quite unpleasant.

Finally everything you take with you will be contained in a rucksack. Make sure it is capacious enough and comfortable to carry when fully loaded: check for correct back length and a snug fit for the load-bearing hip belt. Spare clothing etc can be kept dry in plastic inner bags.

In the unhappy event of an accident, serious injury or illness, or the verified loss of a fellow walker, write down the six-figure map reference of your position and call the police by dialling 999 from the nearest telephone. They will advise the best course of action and if necessary initiate a rescue.

To attract attention in an emergency make the International Distress Call; this is one long signal (a whistle blast, torch flash or similar) every ten seconds for one minute. The answer is three signals per minute, but keep on signalling to guide rescuers towards you.

The most common danger is hypothermia, or exposure. This is caused by a drastic fall in the victim's body temperature, usually due to a combination of cold winds, driving rain (or snow) and sodden clothing. Symptoms include slurred speech, uncharacteristic behaviour such as stumbling and loss of interest in what is happening, pallor and shivering. Insulate the casualty from the ground, get him/her as warm and dry as possible by whatever means are available but don't give alcoholic drinks or rub

Pennine wayfarers, crossing peat bogs on top of Kinder Scout during the first leg, are fully equipped with all they require along the Way (Photograph by Paddy Dillon)

Sheltering in winter, near Kinder Downfall, high above Kinder Reservoir on the first stage of the Way

the skin. Sweet foods such as chocolate can transform the situation but in serious cases medical help is imperative. Exposure can kill!

Avoiding emergencies is infinitely preferable to dealing with them. Know your own fitness level and that of any companions and be prepared to stop early rather than risk an epic.

OBTAINING SUPPLIES AND ACCOMMODATION

Refreshment places such as pubs, cafés and walker-friendly farms are rarely more than a few miles distant wherever you are on the Pennine Way (with one or two exceptions). However, that knowledge may be of little comfort when the going is rough or when you are very tired or fighting a strong headwind. Outside the main summer season some establishments may be open only for restricted hours or closed altogether. Common sense suggests that some sustaining food is carried in addition to emergency rations. On some stretches of trail (eg Edale to Crowden, around Stainmore and in Upper Teesdale, over Cross Fell and the Cheviot) there are no refreshment places at all, so a full day's food or more and in some cases drink too, will need to be packed.

Provisions are obtainable at fairly regular intervals along the Way, with other supplies, banks, post offices, buses etc at the larger villages and towns. The Pennine Way itself passes through relatively few settlements of any size but it is sometimes possible to catch a bus or taxi out and back to the nearest town should the need arise. Assuming you arrive during shop opening hours and that establishments haven't closed down, the following places along the Way can be used to stock up with food items and other basics:

Edale, Crowden, Standedge, Hebden Bridge, Heptonstall, Cowling, Lothersdale, West Marton, Gargrave, Malham, Hawes, Bowes, Horton-in-Ribblesdale, Middleton-in-Teesdale, Dufton, Garrigill, Alston, Bellingham, Byrness and Kirk Yetholm.

Make sure you take enough cash with you – there are not many cash dispensers on the Pennine Way!

The type of accommodation you choose will determine the style of your Pennine Way journey, its cost and to some extent the weight of your rucksack. The Countryside Agency provides a comprehensive Accommodation and Public Transport guide which is available free of charge from The Pennine Way National Trail Officer, The Countryside Agency, 4th Floor Victoria Wharf, No 4 The Embankment, Sovereign Street, Leeds LS1 4BA. Tel: (0113) 246 9222, email: pennineway@countryside.gov.uk.

Leaflets, a completion certificate and much other useful information are also available from www.national-trail.co.uk.

An accommodation guide by the Pennine Way Association is obtainable from local bookshops, tourist information offices or by post from John Needham, 23 Woodland Crescent,

Low Force is passed near Bowlees on the way upstream beside the river Tees, Stage 10
(Photograph by Paddy Dillon)

Hilton Park, Manchester M25 9WQ (current price £1.50 plus an A5 sae).

The Youth Hostels Association operate a Booking Bureau for hostels along the Pennine Way. Contact YHA Booking Bureau, PO Box 6028, Matlock, Derbyshire DE4 3XB. Tel: (0870) 2412314, Fax: (01629) 592627.

Hotels and B&Bs

These are widely used by walkers, though not all are situated exactly on the trail. You are assured of a warm welcome, a hot shower or bath and sustaining food at the beginning and end of the day. Wet clothing and footwear can often be dried out but you will need to carry a spare 'indoor'

outfit. Specifications vary according to price and during the summer season pre-booking is strongly recommended. One disadvantage of this is having to keep up with your self-imposed schedule regardless of adverse weather, injury or fatigue. If arriving at a town without booked accommodation, the tourist information office will usually find you a bed for the night; alternatively try the pubs.

Youth Hostels and Camping

Despite their title, youth hostels these days offer low-cost accommodation for all age groups – some provide meals too. Hostels on or near the Pennine Way are situated at:

Greg's Hut is one option for accommodation

The South Tynedale Railway is gradually extending away from Alston, Stage 11 and 12 (Photograph by Paddy Dillon)

Edale – Rowland Cote, Nether Booth
Tel: (0870) 770 5808

Crowden
Tel: (0870) 770 5784

Mankinholes – Todmorden
Tel: (0870) 770 5952

Haworth
Tel: (0870) 770 5858

Earby – Colne, Lancs
Tel: (0870) 770 5804

Malham
Tel: (0870) 770 5946

Hawes – Lancaster Terrace
Tel: (0870) 770 5854

Keld
Tel: (0870) 770 5888

Baldersdale – Blackton
Tel: (0870) 770 5684

Langdon Beck – Forest-in-Teesdale
Tel: (0870) 770 5910

Dufton – Redstones
Tel: (0870) 770 6113

Alston – The Firs
Tel: (0870) 770 6113

Greenhead
Tel: (0870) 770 6113

Once Brewed – Military Road
Tel: (0870) 770 5980

Bellingham – Woodburn Road
Tel: (0870) 770 5694

Byrness – 7 Otterburn Green
Tel: (01830) 520 425 or
(01629) 592 708
for bookings seven days in advance

Kirk Yetholm
Tel: (0871) 3308 534

In response to the wishes of walkers, bunkhouse accommodation and camping barns are becoming more prevalent. Facilities allow for self-catering and vary from basic to 'all mod cons'. Food may be available from the farm and sleeping bags may sometimes be hired but otherwise must be taken with you.

There are three kinds of camping pitch. Official campsites will usually have showers, washing-up facilities and a shop. Better equipped ones may have washing and drying machines, perhaps even a take-away or café.

Many farms adjacent to the trail are happy to allow lightweight campers to pitch overnight on request (though preferably not large groups). You may get only water and some-where to pitch your tent so you need to be self-sufficient. Farm produce such as eggs and milk are sometimes available.

'Wild' camping by experienced backpackers is feasible in many loca-tions on the Pennine Way but not on open moorland within the Peak National Park, nor in Forestry Commission woodland where there is

High Force is where the River Tees takes a dramatic plunge into a gorge, Stage 10 (Photograph by Paddy Dillon)

a serious risk of fire. Except in emergencies, permission to camp on farmland should always be sought before putting up a tent. Finding sources of clean drinking water can be problematic – farm livestock and sheep often pollute otherwise promising streams so it's wise to carry water sterilising tablets. Needless to say, all litter should be carried away or burned and every care taken to avoid soiling the environment. The backpacker's code is to leave no trace of your stay.

Camping undoubtedly bestows increased flexibility for overnight halts and keeps you more closely in touch with the land and elements. However, it would be folly to set off carrying all the necessary gear without first having become accustomed to the extra pack weight involved and the

techniques for camping successfully in all weathers.

NOTE: Should you wish to park a car in a public place while walking part of the Pennine Way, it is best to contact the nearest tourist information office, or alternatively the police, for advice.

MAPS AND WAYMARKING

Waymarking along the trail takes two main forms: 1) timber fingerposts and plaques bearing the carved words 'Pennine Way'; and 2) the Countryside Agency's acorn symbol which is used on all National Trails. In theory, waymarking should take the guesswork out of navigating through farmland and settlements but in practice this is not always the case. Waymarks themselves are vulnerable to vandalism and accidental damage, they may

A restored Pennine farmhouse in the countryside above Earby, a typical example of other buildings you will see along the Way (Photograph by Paddy Dillon)

become obscured by undergrowth, snow, heavy frost or even parked vehicles, while in mist they may be invisible until you are upon them. And over the moors there are few waymarks at all. It is therefore sensible to carry maps and a compass (and know how to use them!) and to follow this guidebook's directions where necessary.

A map becomes essential should you wander off the trail and become lost, or if you simply need to detour off-route for any reason. The following Ordnance Survey sheets cover the entire Pennine Way:

OS Landranger (1:50,000): Sheets 110, 109, 103, 98, 91, 92, 86, 80 and 74. OS Explorer (1:25,000): Sheets 1, 21, 10, 30, 31, 43, 42 and 16.

Interestingly, with some judicious trimming, the entire set of Landranger maps for the Pennine Way weighs only just over 6oz (184 grams) – an invaluable fund of information and safety to take on the trek.

PLANNING YOUR WALK

Officially the Pennine Way's total length is 268 miles (429km) – 289

The Pennine Way is well sign-posted – here it crosses the Coast to Coast trail near Keld, Stage 9

miles (463km) if all the optional loops are included. But precision is hard to achieve over such long distances, for small twists and turns, wandering off the exact path line and exploring towns, villages and nearby sites of interest all result in a somewhat higher mileage, not to mention diverting off route for refreshments, shopping and accommodation.

The Way has been run in three days! However, most walkers tackling the entire route at one go take around 15 days to complete it at an average 18 miles (29km) per day. The availability of accommodation tends to dictate the distances covered and creates popular, almost inevitable stages. It would be perfectly possible to take three weeks or even longer at a more leisurely pace, enjoying wayside attractions and perhaps building in a few shorter or rest days. Equally, many walkers opt to cover the trail in instalments rather than in a single push. It all boils down to personal inclination and what resources are at your disposal.

If you can select when to walk on the Pennine Way, spring and early summer, along with early autumn are probably the ideal seasons. An influx of tourists and holidaymakers during July and August puts greater pressure on accommodation throughout the Pennine region and the weather then can be less settled. Having said all that, winter expeditions bring their own rewards when the moors are frosty or snow-covered and the bogs frozen hard.

Some preparation in the form of a few weekends of rough walking beforehand and getting accustomed to carrying a loaded rucksack will yield rich dividends. The first stage from Edale to Crowden is something of a baptism by fire and many find it all too easy to become unstuck before the trek has got properly underway. Fitness and equipment need to be up to scratch.

HOW TO USE THIS GUIDE

The Pennine Way has been divided into 16 stages, each ending at a place where accommodation is available. The stages are mostly equivalent to a day's walking, though a few may seem rather on the short or long side. Heading each stage are useful statistics: the distance involved; the main ascents; places on or near the route where refreshments and provisions may be found; access to public transport, if any; types of accommodation on offer (ie B&Bs, youth hostels, campsites and camping barns); and the OS maps (both Landranger and Outdoor Explorer) covering the stage. After a brief summary of what the stage holds in store, there follows a description of the route printed in bold type, with wayside points of interest printed in normal type.

At the end of each stage description appears a list of other trails, mostly long-distance, which connect with the Pennine Way, either intersecting it or in some cases running in tandem with it for part of the stage. The lists do not claim to be definitive

First steps on the trail north from Edale on Stage 1

for new trails are springing up all the time. However, armed with such knowledge it is possible to devise any number of circular or linear walks that use parts of the Pennine Way and parts of other connecting trails. To obtain further details about these trails and their publications, consult the authoritative *Long Distance Walkers' Handbook*, published by A and C Black (current price £9.99).

STAGE 1
Edale to Crowden-in-Longdendale

The first stage may not be the kindest of introductions to a long-distance walk. But any long-distance trek should begin with optimism and there is great inspiration to be gleaned from the Dark Peak's wide horizons and breeze-filled solitude. At the day's end, self-congratulation may be in order at having cracked one of the Way's toughest legs.

Edale, set beneath frowning hillsides at the western end of the Hope valley, is a well-established mecca for walkers of all abilities. You will certainly not feel out of place as you step onto the Pennine Way from a signpost opposite the Old Nag's Head pub at the top of the village.

By any yardstick this stage is a fair day's hike and, unlike many other stretches of the Pennine Way, there is a total absence of refreshment places. Some will inevitably find it gruelling; much will depend on the weather and individual fitness.

In years gone by the Pennine Way was routed north, following the Grinds Brook valley to its head then crossing the Kinder Scout plateau, a forbidding expanse of dissected peat. However, severe erosion problems prompted the authorities to switch the main route to what used to be the alternative bad weather path. It's a rather less traumatic introduction for newcomers to the

Distance:	16 miles (26km)
Main Ascents:	Edale to Kinder Low – 1257ft (383m), Snake Pass to Bleaklow Head – 397ft (121m)
Refreshments: (on/near route)	Edale and Crowden (nothing in between)
Public transport:	Trains to Edale from Manchester and Sheffield. Buses between Manchester and Sheffield pass Crowden-in-Longdendale
Accommodation:	B&Bs, youth hostel, campsites and camping barn at Edale; youth hostel and campsite at Crowden
Maps:	OS Landranger Sheet 110, OS Explorer Sheet 1

Before leaving Edale, be sure to visit the National Park's Fieldhead Information Centre. As well as providing an up-to-date weather forecast and expert advice on local conditions, the Centre houses an informative exhibition and sells maps as well as other accessories.

Dark Peak and the wilder option of a plateau traverse remains open to experienced bog-trotters.

At first the Way meanders along often muddy field paths beneath Broadlee-Bank Tor. The long skyline to the south across the valley is sometimes referred to as The Great Ridge and divides the gritstone Dark Peak from gentler limestone country in the White Peak.

Before long the Way descends gently to a track and Upper Booth Farm. Turn left through the farmyard then right along the tarmac lane above the River Noe. (North to South: turn left off the lane opposite a telephone box). At Lee Farm you'll pass a small National Trust shelter equipped with information boards and benches – a useful shelter in bad weather. Here the tarmac ends and a

The Nag's Head at Edale in Derbyshire is the first pub on the Pennine Way (Photograph by Paddy Dillon)

broad track carries you on north-westwards towards the moortop outcrop of Edale Rocks. →

As the valley head closes in around you, the Way reaches a packhorse bridge and begins climbing sharply up a pitched pathway known as Jacob's Ladder.

As you zig-zag uphill, you are treading in the footsteps of countless trans-Pennine packhorse trains which once carried salt and wool between Cheshire and Yorkshire over these bleak moors. Jacob's Ladder is named after one Jacob Marshall, a packhorse driver who reputedly scrambled up this steep short-cut in order to smoke a pipe while his ponies took the longer alternative track on the left.

There are wonderful views back down the Hope valley from the top of the steep section, after which the stony track continues to gain height steadily. Unless wishing to view Edale Cross, a medieval boundary marker some 300m ahead, turn right at the cairned path junction and follow the peaty ascending path which angles up the flanks of Swine's Back. (From Edale Cross this same point can be reached by following a wall north, then north-east to a wall gap.)

Beyond the conspicuous cairns ahead, aim for the large gritstone outcrop called Edale Rocks. A well-walked path trends away to the north-east here, part of a popular circuit of Kinder's southern edges, but the Pennine Way continues resolutely to the plateau edge just west of Kinder Low trig pillar. (North to South: From Kinder Low bear slightly east of south to Edale Rocks and the clear path down Swine's Back.)

The next 3 miles (5km) provide straightforward, if quite rugged, walking mostly on firm ground as you follow the escarpment edge and cross Red Brook. High above Kinder Reservoir and Hayfield, views extend towards Greater Manchester against a foreground of stunning gritstone scenery sculpted by the elements over aeons of time.

Halfway along this marvellous section, Kinder Downfall is encountered – a spectacular waterfall where the River Kinder plunges over the plateau lip. Spectacular, that is,

Many features like Edale Rocks punctuate the Dark Peak landscapes, often bearing individual names such as Pym Chair, the Wool Packs and Noe Stool.

continued on
page 34

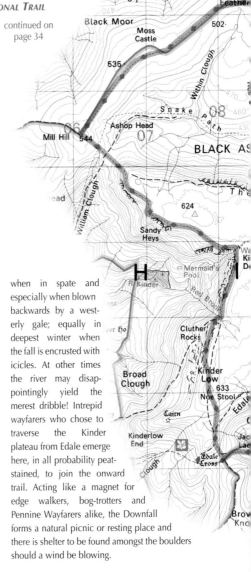

when in spate and especially when blown backwards by a westerly gale; equally in deepest winter when the fall is encrusted with icicles. At other times the river may disappointingly yield the merest dribble! Intrepid wayfarers who chose to traverse the Kinder plateau from Edale emerge here, in all probability peat-stained, to join the onward trail. Acting like a magnet for edge walkers, bog-trotters and Pennine Wayfarers alike, the Downfall forms a natural picnic or resting place and there is shelter to be found amongst the boulders should a wind be blowing.

Staying close to the rugged steepnesses of the plateau rim, the Pennine Way swings north-west. To the east, a soggy, undulating peat wilderness invites the eye but rarely the boot! Before long you have passed Sandy Heys, scene of the 1932 Mass Trespass, and have reached the plateau's westernmost extremity. Here the Way drops abruptly to Ashop Head, a marshy saddle between William Clough and Hayfield on the one hand, and the River Ashop and Woodlands Valley on the other. Linking both valleys, the Snake Path crosses our way at right-angles.

A short climb brings us to Mill Hill and a change of direction to north-east over what was once an arduous 3 miles (5km) of boggy terrain culminating in the infamous Featherbed Moss which was (and still is!) capable of demoralising the strongest walker. Now, however, a long ribbon of flagstones laid to arrest the formation of ever worsening path erosion renders both navigation and forward progress simplicity itself – except perhaps in wet or icy conditions when the stone surface can become slippery.

Rediscovery of the traditional 'causey' or 'flag path' as a long-term solution to erosion problems has revolutionised the management of many stretches on the Pennine Way and other National Trails. Mill flags from demolition sites are air-lifted to each location in special tipper cages slung beneath a helicopter.

The original stone causeys

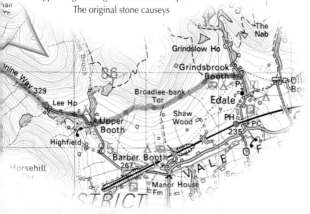

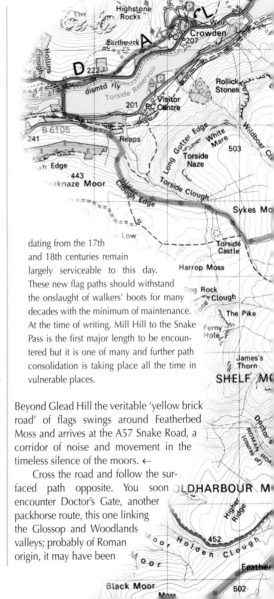

dating from the 17th and 18th centuries remain largely serviceable to this day. These new flag paths should withstand the onslaught of walkers' boots for many decades with the minimum of maintenance. At the time of writing, Mill Hill to the Snake Pass is the first major length to be encountered but it is one of many and further path consolidation is taking place all the time in vulnerable places.

The Snake Road owes its name not to its convolutions but to the serpent incorporated into the Cavendish family crest – former landowners hereabouts – as does the Snake Inn some 3 miles (5km) down to the east. Not surprisingly the Snake Pass is often the first road in the region to be blocked by winter snows.

Beyond Glead Hill the veritable 'yellow brick road' of flags swings around Featherbed Moss and arrives at the A57 Snake Road, a corridor of noise and movement in the timeless silence of the moors. ←

Cross the road and follow the surfaced path opposite. You soon encounter Doctor's Gate, another packhorse route, this one linking the Glossop and Woodlands valleys; probably of Roman origin, it may have been named after a sixteenth-century Glossop vicar who frequently travelled along it.

Ahead up the shallow trench of Devil's Dyke the going can be squelchy and some walkers prefer the banktop either side. At the top end follow the way-marked, twisting peat channel which swings north-west and meets the deeper little valley of Hern Clough. The onward path, flagstoned in places and waymarked with occasional posts, criss-crosses the stream and passes the Hern Stones over to the west. Eventually you are walking in the gravelly stream bed itself, then in winding peat groughs before finally emerging onto the 'moonscape' of the Bleaklow plateau. Close by are the Wain Stones, from certain angles resembling two primitive heads about to kiss. Aiming just east of north you will locate the large cairn at Bleaklow Head from where a bearing north-north-west leads off to the initially rather tentative descent path. Having found it brings a flush of relief to most Pennine Wayfarers for Bleaklow is no place in which to get lost, especially if the weather is poor. Although sandy and rocky in the immediate vicinity, a vast peaty wilderness broods on all sides, ready to entrap the errant walker. (North to South: After reaching Bleaklow Head cairn, walk south-south-east to find the way-marked peat grough then the stream bed down into Hern Clough.)

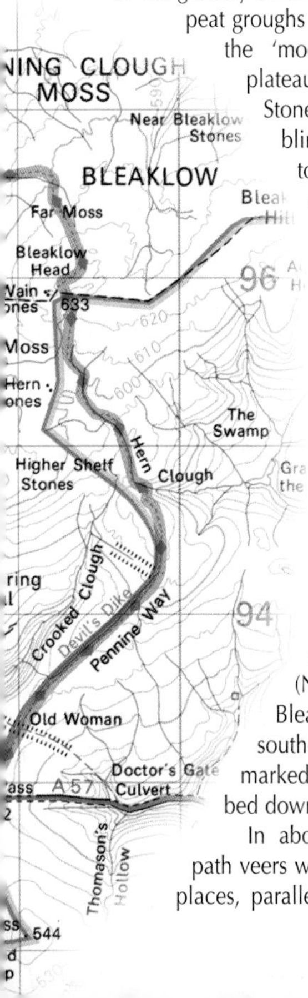

In about 15 minutes the onward path veers west and continues, flagged in places, parallel to the miniature valley of

(Map labels, left margin, reading approximately top to bottom:) WING CLOUGH MOSS · Near Bleaklow Stones · BLEAKLOW · Far Moss · Bleaklow Head · Wain Stones 633 · Moss · Hern Stones · The Swamp · Higher Shelf Stones · Hern Clough · ring · Crooked Clough · Devil's Dyke · Pennine Way · Old Woman · Doctor's Gate Culvert · A57 · Thomason's Hollow · 544

Wildboar Grain. Lower down at the confluence with Torside Clough lies John Track Well, a rather secretive walled spring once used by packhorse trains. Cross over here and climb the steep bank onto a path partly flagged and partly very muddy, rising high along Clough Edge, the southern rim of Torside Clough. Heralding a return to civilisation after the rigours of Kinder and Bleaklow, it drops steeply to Reaps Farm. At the bottom turn left down a sunken track then over grass to join the farm lane.

Having crossed an old railway trackbed (part of the Longdendale Trail) and the B6105, walk down to the

Pennine Wayfareers high up the rugged Grindsbrook Clough on Kinder Scout (Photograph by Paddy Dillon)

dam between Torside and Rhodeswood reservoirs and at the far end climb steps on your right into a permissive bridleway through a conifer plantation. Ahead cross the busy A628 and follow the gently rising track opposite. Further on at a finger post the Pennine Way turns left but the majority of walkers will be more interested in reaching Crowden youth hostel or campsite for a well-earned night's rest and recuperation. Both lie a short distance straight on along the track.

Dry conditions near Kinder Low make for easy going

OTHER CONNECTING TRAILS

Longdendale Trail: Above Torside Reservoir near the stage's end, the Pennine Way crosses the Longdendale Trail. This is a North West Water route along a disused railway trackbed from Hadfield to Woodhead Tunnel, part of the 200 mile (320km) multi-use Trans-Pennine Trail for walkers, cyclists and, where feasible, horse riders, which runs coast-to-coast from Merseyside to Hull. Many sections of the trail utilise old railway trackbeds but despite being part-urban, quite significant stretches cross open countryside. When completed, the Trans-Pennine Trail will become part of the E8 European long-distance path.

*Pennine Wayfarers
passing the Kinder
Gates rock outcrops on
Kinder Scout
(Photograph by Paddy
Dillon)*

Start: Southport, Merseyside (SD 338172)
Finish: Hornsea, Humberside (TA 208479)
OS Landranger Sheets: 105, 106, 107, 108, 109, 110, 111
Waymarks: Disc bearing trail logo.

Dark Peak Boundary Walk: A tough, 78 miles (125km) high-level circuit on moors, gritstone edges, wooded cloughs, reservoirs and villages.
Start and Finish: Hayfield, Derbyshire (SK 037869)
OS Landranger Sheet: 110

Peak District High Level Route: Exceptionally strenuous, this 91 mile (145km) route takes in the White Peak plateau, Kinder Scout and the eastern gritstone edges.
Start and Finish: Matlock, Derbyshire (SK 298603)
OS Landranger Sheets: 110, 119

Dark Peak Challenge Walk: A testing, 24 miles (38km) high-level circuit over gritstone moors and edges.
Start and Finish: Hathersage, Derbyshire (SK 232815)
OS Landranger Sheet: 119

Peakland Way: John Merrill's 97 mile (155km) circuit includes limestone dales, Kinder Scout and ends along the Tissington Trail.

Start and Finish: Ashbourne, Derbyshire (SK 178469)
OS Landranger Sheets: 110, 119

Ramblers Way: This 38 mile (61km) route visits sites of the famous mass trespasses that began the fight for public access to these hills. A strenuous walk over Kinder Scout and adjacent hills and ending along Stanage Edge.
Start: Castleton, Derbyshire (SK 150829)
Finish: Hathersage, Derbyshire (SK 232815)
OS Landranger Sheet: 110

STAGE 2
Crowden-in-Longdendale to Standedge

Kinder and Bleaklow may be fading memories but this stage too traverses peaty moorland. Even on notorious Black Hill, however, the groughs are tame compared with Bleaklow's miniature canyons! Some relief from the high, sombre moors is gained in the Wessenden Valley – a delightful interlude – before once again the Pennine Way strikes uphill. Reaching Standedge may seem like a short day, but accommodation is available nearby and many wayfarers will welcome the opportunity to recover from residual fatigue and to 'shake down' into the walking. Besides, Standedge represents the northern perimeter of the Peak National Park – a tidy statistic! Beyond lie many more miles of moortop before the next natural break.

Back at the finger post above Crowden, the Pennine Way strikes north on a clear though rough path gradually ascending the valley of Crowden Great Brook. As the Way approaches the valley's western escarpment you will encounter a couple of steeper gradients before

Distance:	12 miles (19.5km)
Main Ascents:	Crowden to Black Hill – 1116ft (340m), Wessenden Lodge to Black Moss Reservoir – 361ft (110m)
Refreshments: (on/near route)	Crowden; 'Snoopy's' snack bar at the A635; Globe Farm and The Eagles Nest pub at Standedge
Public transport:	Buses for Marsden (nearest railway station) and Oldham pass Globe Farm, Standedge
Accommodation:	Youth hostel and campsite at Crowden-in-Longdendale; B&B and camping at Globe Farm, Standedge
Maps:	OS Landranger Sheet 110, OS Explorer Sheet 1

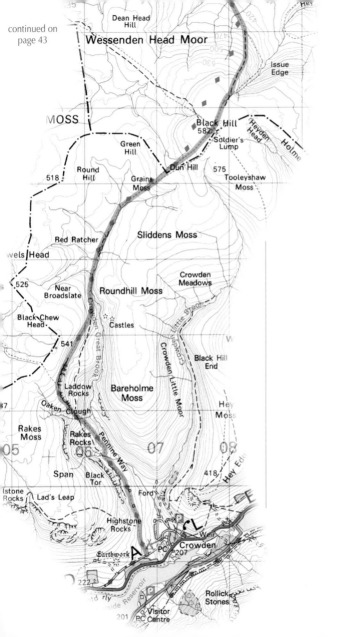

continued on
page 43

Dean Head
Hill

Wessenden Head Moor

Issue
Edge

MOSS

Black Hill
582

Heyden
Head

Holme

Green
Hill

Soldier's
Lump

Round
Hill

Dun Hill

575

Tooleyshaw
Moss

518

Grains
Moss

Red Ratcher

Sliddens Moss

wels Head

Crowden
Meadows

525

Near
Broadslate

Roundhill Moss

Black Chew
Head

Castles

541

Crowden Little Moor

Little Brook

Crowden Great Brook

Black Hill
End

Laddow
Rocks

Bareholme
Moss

Oaken Clough

Hey
Moss

Rakes
Moss

Rakes
Rocks

Pennine Way

07

08

Span

Black
Tor

418

Hey Edge

Istone
Rocks

Lad's Leap

Ford

05

06

Highstone
Rocks

P

Weir

Earthwork

PC

Crowden
207

Rollick
Stones

222

d rly

side Reservoir

P

201

Visitor
PC Centre

41

crossing the rocky bed of Oakenclough Brook and rising to the edge of high moorland above Laddow Rocks.

As you climb away from Longdendale, take a look back now and then. This important corridor through the Pennines carries communications between Sheffield and Manchester as it has since the Middle Ages when Cheshire salt, among other commodities, was exported to Yorkshire by packhorse. A turnpike road was built in 1731 (now the busy A628); the road outlived the railway whose gravel trackbed is converted for use as the Longdendale Trail. Reservoirs providing Manchester's water date from 1862 and dominate the valley.

During the early 20th century this gritstone edge enjoyed immense popularity with Manchester climbers – part of the original movement which pioneered climbing as a sport in Britain. With care it is possible for walkers to clamber down to a cave below an overhang at the northern end for a better view of the cracks, chimneys and walls that are not visible from above.

Although a path continues north-west from a small cairn to Chew Reservoir and Greenfield, the Pennine Way stays close to the escarpment edge reaching 1640ft (500m) above Laddow Rocks. ←

The onward path now loses height and converges with Crowden Great Brook. (North to South: Be sure to keep up right here rather than stray onto an old disused low-level path.) Criss-crossing the stream several times, the Way becomes increasingly tortuous but is flagged over the once infamously squelchy approaches to Black Hill. From Dun Hill (the county boundary between Derbyshire and Yorkshire), the trail presses on to the delights of Black Hill summit!

This desolate place was dubbed 'Soldier's Lump' after the rigours endured by the original Royal Engineers triangulation team. The morass of bare peat is now crossed by flags and the once often unreachable, eroded trig pillar has been restored to normal status. There is a strong sense or remoteness here yet the nearest road is only 1¼ miles (2.5km) away east-south-east in the direction of Holme Moss TV masts which date from 1951.

Over past decades many were the struggles with deep, glutinous peat on Black Hill. Today however, thanks to the installation of flagstones, the going is mercifully firm and clear, even in the worst conditions (deep snow excepted!).

The trail is sparsely cairned east of north off Black Hill and an eventually clear path leads down to Black Dike Head, to the west of Issue Clough. Peat groughs on the flanks of Wessenden Head Moor are relieved by

The eroded summit of Black Hill in pre-flagstone days

welcome flagstones as you swing north-west and cross feeder streams, including the larger defile of Dean Clough.

Already in sight unless the mist is down, the A635 provides a respite from the empty country just traversed and signals a shift, at least temporarily, to gentler scenery in the Wessenden Valley.

Since the recommended Pennine Way from Black Hill changed to the Wessenden route, so did the point at which it bisects the A635. Happily, 'Snoopy's' refreshment caravan also moved station and at the time of writing stands opposite the Meltham Road turn-off near the site of the old Isle of Skye Inn, demolished, so the story goes, to 'protect water purity in the Wessenden reservoirs'!

Turn right alongside the A635 for about 150m then follow the minor road opposite; at the first right-hand bend turn left onto a good reservoir track. The going is straightforward, passing Wessenden Head Reservoir and continuing north-west round hillsides to Wessenden

Lodge beside the lower reservoir. Follow the signs past Wessenden Lodge and bear left across the valley. Walk up to a waterfall and cross Shiny Brook at the small weir (which can be a little awkward with a large rucksack in wet weather). Now follow the onward path swinging west into Blakely Clough. Once over the stream bed a quite rough and peaty ascent leads up onto Black Moss. More peat groughs, some quite large, flank the partly flagged path weaving between Swellands and Black Moss reservoirs. At the latter both old and newer routes from Black Hill rejoin along a sandy track. An easy descent ensues on a flag path towards Redbrook Reservoir, veering west along the old packhorse road to the A62 which is reached near a small car park at Standedge Cutting. Pub and accommodation lie down to your left within walking distance; the only viable alternatives are further on and well off-route.

The Pack Horse Inn as seen from near the Lower Gorple Reservoir (Photograph by Paddy Dillon)

OTHER CONNECTING TRAILS

Kirklees Way: From the A635 down the Wessenden Valley to Wessenden Lodge, the Pennine Way runs in tandem with the Kirklees Way. This is a 73 mile (116km) trail set up by Kirklees Metropolitan Council that forms a large circle around Huddersfield, taking in both high moortops and industrial valley towns.
Start and Finish: Scholes, West Yorkshire (SE 167259)
OS Landranger Sheets: 104, 110
Waymarks: Discs bearing a blue letter 'K'

Cuckoo Walk: A tough circuit of often boggy moorland, taking in Black Hill and White Moss. 18 miles (29km).
Start and Finish: Marsden, West Yorkshire (SE 049116)
OS Landranger Sheet: 110

Ten Reservoirs Walk: A strenuous circuit over the Saddleworth Moors, linking with the Pennine Way at Black Moss, Swellands and Wessenden reservoirs. 22 miles (35km).
Start and Finish: Dovestone Reservoir, Greater Manchester (SE 014034)
OS Landranger Sheet: 110

STAGE 3
Standedge to Calderdale

Although this stage does encounter some boggy stretches, these are insignificant compared with those already endured! Gritstone edges and lofty moors ahead are interrupted at first by little more than trans-Pennine roads. Paths on the whole are better surfaced, although a long middle section of level reservoir tracks may be anathema to some. These South Pennine moors, less well walked than other better known areas, are nonetheless elemental and spirit-lifting. Their windswept tops, flanked by hill farms, dales, towns and villages redolent with social and industrial history, provide marvellous walking country. Little wonder they have inspired such well-known poets and writers as Ted Hughes and the Bronte sisters. The Pennine Way, however, merely flirts with things man-made – the occasional road, aerial mast, trig pillar or reservoir – until it dives into Calderdale at the end of the stage.

From the car park near Little Brun Clough Reservoir, cross the A62 Manchester to Huddersfield road and follow the sandy track opposite, bearing left then right

Distance:	15 miles (24.5km)
Main Ascents:	M62 to Blackstone Edge – 260ft (80m)
Refreshments: (on/near route)	Snack bar usually at A672 near Windy Hill; The White House Inn on A58 near Blackstone Reservoir (possibly open only for lunches and dinners); all shops and services in Hebden Bridge.
Public transport:	Buses and trains to Manchester, Liverpool and Leeds.
Accommodation:	Youth hostel at Mankinholes, near Todmorden; B&Bs at Charlestown and Hebden Bridge.
Maps:	OS Landranger Sheets 110, 109 and 103, OS Explorer Sheet 21

Before leaving Standedge for good, spare a thought for the 'navvies' who excavated 3 miles (5km) of railway and canal tunnels through the bedrock beneath the cutting, thus linking Greater Manchester with West Yorkshire. The railway tunnel is still in use and the canal tunnel, Britain's longest, is once again open to narrowboats after many years of closure. There is a visitor's centre.

on a waymarked path up onto Millstone Edge. Incidentally, both the Oldham Trail and the Standedge Trail are joined here for a while. ←

Weathered gritstone frames the rugged hillsides descending west to Diggle and Oldham and you soon reach a trig pillar at 1470ft (448m). Nearby stands a memorial stone to the Saddleworth poet, Ammon Wrigley, who died in 1946.

At the top of Cudworth Clough the Oldham Way forks left, but the Pennine Way bears right on a well-made path over and down to Oldgate Moss. Cross the A640 Rochdale to Huddersfield road, originally a packhorse route, and follow the Way opposite, rising at first over Rape Hill. After dipping through Readycon Dean, it climbs again, passing the trig pillar on White Hill at 1529ft (466m).

Early morning on Millstone Edge

continued on page 51

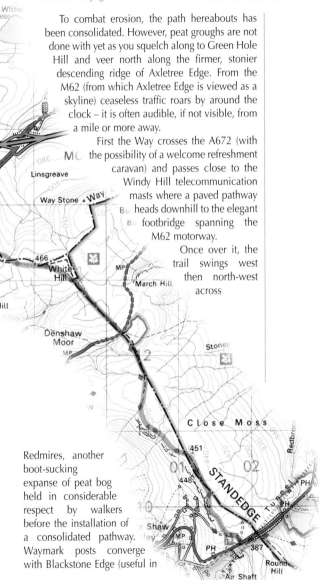

To combat erosion, the path hereabouts has been consolidated. However, peat groughs are not done with yet as you squelch along to Green Hole Hill and veer north along the firmer, stonier descending ridge of Axletree Edge. From the M62 (from which Axletree Edge is viewed as a skyline) ceaseless traffic roars by around the clock – it is often audible, if not visible, from a mile or more away.

First the Way crosses the A672 (with the possibility of a welcome refreshment caravan) and passes close to the Windy Hill telecommunication masts where a paved pathway heads downhill to the elegant footbridge spanning the M62 motorway.

Once over it, the trail swings west then north-west across

Redmires, another boot-sucking expanse of peat bog held in considerable respect by walkers before the installation of a consolidated pathway. Waymark posts converge with Blackstone Edge (useful in mist) where the trig pillar perches atop a huge rock at 1549ft (472m). Gritstone blocks, boulders and slabs proliferate and there are distant urban views here where the Pennine Way squeezes through the narrowest corridor of moorland between the conurbations of Greater Manchester and Huddersfield. Easier going soon ensues on a gradual descent to the Aiggin Stone (pronounced 'Aijin'), an old boundary marker. Here you turn left down a stretch of 'Roman Road'. There's ambiguity about its origins for although flagged and paved in Roman style, it may equally have been constructed for packhorses.

After about 300m turn right along a contouring path beside Broad Head Drain. This leat curves round Blackstone Edge Moor to a quarry where a left turn downhill brings you out to the A58 Littleborough to Sowerby Bridge road. Turn right and cross the road by the White House Inn (disappointingly not open all day at the time of writing) then turn left onto a reservoir road.

The Pennine Way now enters reservoir country with a vengeance! Walking is along good, level tracks for almost 3 miles (5km) but this can be hard on the feet. First Blackstone Edge Reservoir then Light Hazzles and Warland reservoirs are passed, their water levels dependent upon recent weather conditions.

> It is a breezy, expansive landscape of water and rolling heather moorland set above the densely populated valley containing Littleborough and Todmorden to the west. Held in the valley bottom is the Rochdale Canal, completed in 1804; the reservoirs were then built to supply water to the canal.

Eventually the northern end of Warland Reservoir is reached and the trail continues beside Warland Drain, veering sharp right (east-south-east) then arcing gradually north-eastwards to an acute bend. The waymarked trail now heads off due north across Coldwell Hill, with Stoodley Pike Monument in view. It is well known among Pennine Wayfarers that the monument's size

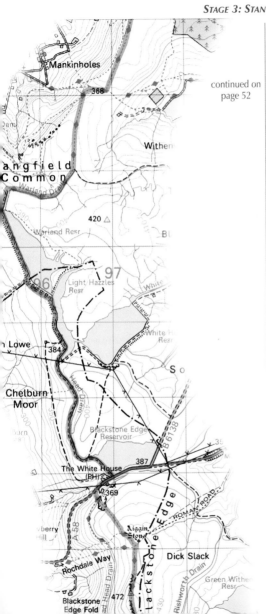

continued on
page 52

51

(125ft (38m) high) deceives the eye into thinking it is nearer than it actually is. Most laden walkers will take the better part of an hour to reach it from its first sighting.

At Withens Gate you cross the Calderdale Way (Mankinholes youth hostel lies down to the west) and finally approach Stoodley Pike Monument, one of the Pennine's best-known landmarks. ←

Heading east the trail now begins a 2¼ mile (4.5km) descent into the busy Calderdale Valley. Beyond a spring of drinking water and a wall, a ladder stile leads you down left past the Doe Stones to meet a track near Swillington Farm. Carry on downhill, turning

Started originally to celebrate peace following Napoleon's exile to Elba in 1814, work on the monument was postponed when he subsequently escaped the following year. After his defeat in 1815 at the Battle of Waterloo, the monument was finally completed, only to collapse 40 years later! Today's more durable successor dates from 1856.

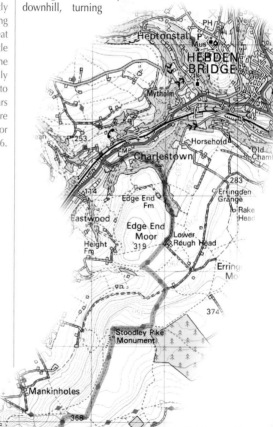

Stoodley Pike

right across a couple of fields to reach the access lane at Rough Head Farm. Trending north, this enters pretty Callis Wood, the first trees for many a mile. Lower down watch for a footpath on the right cutting off a bend and rejoin the access lane down to a bridge over the River Calder and the Rochdale Canal.

The shops, services, refreshment places and accommodation of Hebden Bridge lie a mile along to the right, reached by a canalside path to Black Pit Lock. The town is an important supply point for campers (though the Pennine Way itself misses it out altogether) and represents an opportunity for walkers of every inclination to sample a few civilised indulgences after three days spent tramping the high moors.

Calderdale's abundance of soft, swiftly-flowing water led to the development of a thriving textile industry from the 16th to the early 20th centuries. It shaped the lives of generations and left its marks permanently on the landscape. Valley bottom towns such as Hebden Bridge

Looking west above Globe Farm, Standedge

drew their workforce from surrounding hillside villages when steam power and large mills took over from hand processing. From modest beginnings as simply a river crossing on the old way between Burnley and Halifax, the town became an industrial centre, its great mills on the flat valley floor, housing for workers stacked along the steep hillsides.

Eventually Hebden Bridge's fortunes declined. In more recent times it has adapted to change by accommodating small scale, modern industries and by establishing itself as a historical showpiece, a focus for Pennine arts and crafts and a welcoming tourist destination. The self-guided Town Trail using a booklet available from the tourist information office is well worth following if time allows.

In 1978, the 50 mile (80km) Calderdale Way was opened, providing a circular walk which explores the many facets of this archetypal Pennine valley – its wild flanking moorland, old mills and paved causeys, its ancient halls, laithe houses and weaving hamlets, its hill farms and bustling towns.

OTHER CONNECTION TRAILS

Oldham Way: At Standedge and along Millstone Edge the Pennine Way joins the Oldham Way, a 40 mile (64km) circular route on moorland and urban paths round Oldham.
Start and Finish: Dove Stone Reservoir, Greenfield (SE 002036)
OS Landranger Sheets: 109, 110
Waymarks: Owl logo

Station to Station Walk: Not far beyond Millstone Edge where the Pennine Way crosses the A640, it intersects the 12 mile (19km) Station to Station Walk linking Littleborough and Marsden railway stations.

New Five Trig Points Walk: This 18 mile (29km) route uses lanes, tracks and paths over the Pennine moors connecting five trig pillars, including those on Millstone Edge, White Hill and Blackstone Edge.
Start and Finish: Delph, Greater Manchester (SD 985079)
OS Landranger Sheets: 109, 110

Recedham Way: A 50 mile (80km) circuit following the former parish boundary of Rochdale, joining the Pennine Way from White Hill to Warland Reservoir. Varied terrain from moorland to wooded valleys.
Start and Finish: Marland, Rochdale, Greater Manchester
OS Landranger Sheets: 103, 109

Calderdale Way: At Withens Gate above Mankinhole, the Pennine Way intersects the Calderdale Way, a 50 mile (80km) clockwise circuit of this West Yorkshire valley. The trail takes in moorside villages and the mill towns of Halifax, Hebden Bridge and Todmorden. It was opened in 1978 and utilises many hillside stretches of old packhorse causeys. Designated link routes enable shorter sections of the trail to be incorporated into circular walks.

Start and Finish: Greetland, West Yorkshire (SE 097214)
OS Landranger Sheets: 103, 104, 110
Waymarks: Calderdale Way trefoil

Greater Manchester Boundary Walk: A large clockwise circuit round Manchester. The 130 mile (208km) trail covers a mix of lowland and moorland terrain and offers much scenic variety.
Start and Finish: Woolley Bridge, Greater Manchester (SE 008958)
OS Landranger Sheets: 108, 109, 110

Pennine Bridleway: The Mary Towneley loop is now waymarked and open.

STAGE 4
Calderdale to Lothersdale

Intricate paved paths characterise the departure from Calderdale. Thereafter the stage is once again dominated by moorland: not just any moorland however, for here west of Haworth the heights, Wuthering or otherwise, have been immortalised by the famous Bronte sisters. Almost inevitably there are reservoirs too, but the walking has a gentler flavour in places, as if anticipating the verdant, more hospitable country that lies ahead.

Road, river, canal and railway crowd the valley floor in Calderdale and the air may temporarily lack the purity you have grown accustomed to thus far on the Pennine Way! But escape is close at hand: just along to the right on the opposite side of the A646, the trail heads up

Distance:	18¼ miles (30km)
Main Ascents:	Charlestown to Heptonstall Moor – 886ft (270m); Graining Water to Withins Height – 525ft (160m); Ponden Reservoir to Ickornshaw Moor – 623ft (190m); Ickornshaw village to above Lothersdale – 302ft (92m)
Refreshments: (on/near route)	Highgate Farm shop, Colden; Ponden Hall (seasonal); Black Bull pub, A6068 near Cowling
Public transport:	The Worth Valley Railway (privately run) stops at Haworth, 2 miles (3.2km) east of Ponden for connection with main line trains at Keighley; buses from Cowling to Colne (nearest railway station).
Accommodation:	B&Bs at Colden, Blackshaw Head, Ponden Hall, Cowling, Ickornshaw and Lothersdale; nearest youth hostels are Haworth and Colne; camping at New Delight pub (Colden), High Greenwood House (Heptonstall), Upper Heights Farm, Ponden Hall, Winter House Farm (Cowling)
Maps:	OS Landranger Sheet 103, OS Explorer Sheet 21

Underbank Avenue beneath an old Lancashire and Yorkshire Railway bridge and into a footpath past cottages leading to a junction by a curious ruined chapel. The official way turns right here, though there is provision for Alfred Wainwright's alternative keeping left.

Contouring at first then rising along neglected hillside, there are wonderful views back over to Stoodley Pike. Beyond steps at a little stone-faced waterfall, the trail passes round farm buildings and enters a walled track to reach a junction. Bear left and in 100m turn right through a wall gap to head north up rectangular fields enclosed in the late 18th century. Once across Badger Lane and over Pry Hill there is a heather-lined descent through the upper reaches of Colden Clough. Colden Water itself is spanned by an old stone packhorse bridge at an intersection with the Calderdale Way here in the wooded, rocky recesses of Hebble Hole. Climbing steeply out, the trail curves left to by-pass Goose Hey Farm then resumes northward progress to Colden hamlet at the Burnley to Hebden Bridge road.

A short distance ahead, cross Edge Lane. (Should items of shopping be required, High Gate Farm shop can be found about 250m along to the left – a veritable Aladdin's Cave serving the local community as well as passing walkers.)

Past Long High Top and Mount Pleasant farms, the Way ascends, steeply at first, onto the broad open expanses of Heptonstall Moor. From the shallow summit of Clough Head Hill a generally north-westerly course takes you round the eastern slopes of Standing Stone Hill and down to a track onto which you turn right to pass Gorple Cottages near Gorple Lower Reservoir.

On down a paved path lies the confluence of Reaps

continued on page 60

Water and Graining Water; these are tributaries of Hebden Water whose deeply wooded dale meanders past Hardcastle Crags on its way to join Crimsworth Dean Beck and the River Calder. Ahead footbridges span the streams in a miniature ravine, then the paved trail rises along the east bank of Graining Water to meet the Hebden Bridge – Brierfield road. Turn left and once past Well Hole Cottage turn right, just past the Gorple Reservoir service road opposite. A path quickly leads you to the concrete reservoir roadway serving Walshaw Dean. Bear right before the first reservoir and follow its east bank to the dam separating the lower and middle reservoirs.

Rhododendrons have colonised the shore, though elsewhere bushes and trees are in short supply hereabouts. Having crossed a footbridge by the dam, the onward trail takes to a path as far as a bridge

continued on
page 62

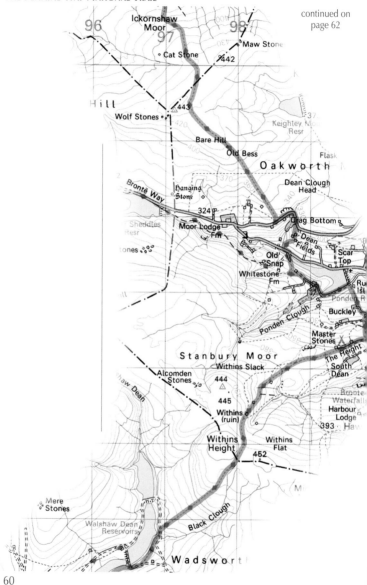

Ickornshaw
Moor

96   97   98

Maw Stone

Cat Stone   442

443

Hill   Wolf Stones

Bare Hill

Old Bess   Oakworth

Flask

Bronte Way   Keighley M
Resr

Dean Clough
Head

Hanging
Stone

324   Crag Bottom

Sheddles
Resr   Moor Lodge   Dean
Fm   Fields   Scar
Top

ones   Old
Snap

Whitestone
Fm   Ponden R

Buckley

Ponden Clough   Master
Stones

The Height

Stanbury Moor   South
Dean

Withins Slack

haw Dean   Alcomden
Stones   444

445   Bronte
Waterfall

Withins
(ruin)   Harbour
Lodge

Withins   393   Hav
Height   Withins
Flat

452

Mere
Stones

Black Clough

Walshaw Dean
Reservoirs   Wadswort

Charlotte Brontë's Chair on the moorland slopes below Top Withens
(Photograph by Paddy Dillon)

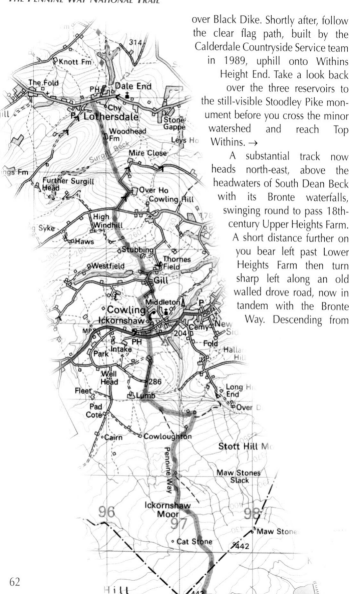

over Black Dike. Shortly after, follow the clear flag path, built by the Calderdale Countryside Service team in 1989, uphill onto Withins Height End. Take a look back over the three reservoirs to the still-visible Stoodley Pike monument before you cross the minor watershed and reach Top Withins. →

A substantial track now heads north-east, above the headwaters of South Dean Beck with its Bronte waterfalls, swinging round to pass 18th-century Upper Heights Farm. A short distance further on you bear left past Lower Heights Farm then turn sharp left along an old walled drove road, now in tandem with the Bronte Way. Descending from the moors into the Worth Valley with its chequered hill-sides of field patterns, the trail jinks right to Buckley Green then left towards Buckley House cottages where a waymarked path on the right drops via Rush Isles Farm to Ponden Reservoir.

With Haworth's accommodation, shops and attractions just 2 miles (3.5km) along the road to the east, this stage could be shortened, especially for those interested in the Bronte story. Many Pennine Wayfarers, however, will have sights set on reaching Cowling or Lothersdale and will know from the map that one more block of moorland lies ahead.

First follow the reservoir shoreline track to Ponden Hall (another possible overnight stop which may also offer refreshments in the holiday season). Dating from 1680, the hall has been associated with Emily Bronte's Thrushcross Grange. Passing outbuildings, the trail contours well above the reservoir until an acute right turn brings you down to a bridge over the River Worth at the Colne – Haworth road.

A short but complicated section begins from a ladder stile just along to the west. First climb parallel to Dean Clough over Dean Fields, guided by old gateposts. Keep left beyond a ruined barn, pass a house to your right and follow a walled farm track. Watch out for a sharp left turn and follow the line of a wall above the shady depths of Dean Clough to meet the road at Crag Bottom. Swinging round the little valley, it reaches Old Crag Bottom Farm where the Pennine Way turns off right and climbs to Crag Top; in good visibility it's a splendid viewpoint over Bronte country.

This spot also signals the start of this stage's final moorland crossing and as you steadily gain height north-westwards beside wall and fence, surroundings change from pasture and farm to the familiar austerity of bilberry, heather, wet grasses and increasing exposures of peat. Bearing slightly left from Old Bess Hill above Keighley Moor Reservoir, the Way is clear enough on the ground as it threads through wet, boggy areas. To the east rise the Wolf Stones with their crowning trig pillar at 1453ft (443m).

Occupied until the 1930s, the lonely farmstead of Top Withins crumbled into a ruin, which was however still entirely in keeping with the wild and romantic vision of Emily Bronte, whose Wuthering Heights may well have been inspired by this spot. Unfortunately, by consolidating the site as a shrine for the many thousands of literary pilgrims who come here from all over the world, that elusive, evocative essence has, perhaps inevitably, been lost.

Trending north towards distant Cowling Parish Church, you gradually begin to lose height from Cat Stone Hill over the peaty sweep of Ickornshaw Moor, whose peat groughs, though alleviated by flagstones, make an unwelcome reappearance. ←

From a stone hut on High End Lowe, the path meets a wall and passes several small timber-built chalets before veering left. Further down at the end of the wall you follow marker posts to a ladder stile.

Reference to wolves and cats on these moors remind us of a period in history three or four centuries past when such wild species roamed the countryside, slowly lost their ground to farmers and hunters and eventually retreated to the high moortops for sanctuary.

As well as a return to more hospitable terrain, there are views on this stretch of two conspicuous monuments: Wainman's Pinnacle on the edge of Earl Crag, possibly, argue historians, commemorating the Battle of Waterloo; and Lund's Tower, a folly put up to celebrate Queen Victoria's Golden Jubilee by James Lund of Malsis Hall.

The gradient steepens in an area of ruinous farmsteads and after crossing Andrew Gutter the Way contours round Eller Hill to the waterfall at Lumb Head. Curving north, the trail takes a walled track and green lane down to Lower Summer House farm with its miscellany of livestock. Below, a track then a field path lead out to the A6068 near Ickornshaw village.

Turn left then, just before the Black Bull pub, turn down right and at the lower road turn right again. The Way now bears left past the church, heading roughly northwards to Middleton's terraced houses, joining Gill Lane which descends to cross Gill Bridge in a delightful wooded hollow. Once over you turn sharp left then right up hillside meadows near Low Stubbing. Straightforward field paths lead up to the left of High Stubbing and on to Cowling Hill Lane. Almost opposite to the right, take the lane past Over House and at a sharp right bend keep straight on over a stile. With no complications the Way drops to cross Surgill Beck, rises again to pass Woodhead Farm and finally forks right to descend sharply down by a wall into Lothersdale.

Snuggling in a deep cleft of the hills, Lothersdale remains hidden until you are almost upon it, its preserved textile

Lothersdale

mill chimney peeping first into view. There are B&Bs here, as well as a pub – the Hare and Hounds – a post office and several groups of distinctive old houses. The village represents the end of a long succession of bleak and, at times, arduous moorland crossings; wounds can now be licked in anticipation of easy-going, pastoral walking in Craven and Airedale on the threshold of the Yorkshire Dales.

OTHER CONNECTING TRAILS

Haworth to Hebden Bridge Walk: This 9 mile (14.5km) route is coincident with the Pennine Way between Walshaw Dean Middle Reservoir and Top Withins.

Bronte Way: Extended in 1992, this popular 40 mile (64km) route joins the Pennine Way on the descent into the Worth valley and along Ponden Reservoir's south shore. The trail draws in most of the sites associated with the Bronte family.
Start: Gawthorpe Hall, Lancashire (SD 805340)
Finish: Oakwell Hall, West Yorkshire (SE 217271)

OS Landranger Sheets: 103, 104
Waymarks: Posts bearing the Bronte Way name.

Bronte Round: Another, shorter route on moorland, riverside and farmland paths linking the main Bronte sites. 23 miles (37km).
Start and Finish: Hebden Bridge, West Yorkshire (SD 992272)
OS Landranger Sheets: 103, 104

Watersheds Walk: A 25 miles (40km) high-level circuit of the moors around the Worth valley.
Start and Finish: Keighley Railway Station, West Yorkshire (SE 065413)
OS Landranger Sheet: 104

Trans-Pennine Walk: A high quality, scenic route of 54 miles (87km) linking the western Lancashire Pennines with Yorkshire's Bronte Country to the east. The trail joins the Pennine Way from Stoodley Pike to Hebden Bridge and again at Top Withins en route for Haworth.
Start: Adlington, Lancashire (SD 610130)
Finish: Haworth, West Yorkshire (SE 030372)
OS Landranger Sheets: 103, 104, 109

STAGE 5
Lothersdale to Malham

A climb over Pinhaw Beacon reveals extensive views, most exciting of which are the limestone hills around Malham along the northern horizon. But first there is a gentle descent towards the fertile Aire valley, a green and pleasant interlude. With plenty of refreshment places along the way and only undulating field paths to deal with, walking is relaxed through pastoral, lowland landscapes, at times beside canal or river.

After passing the Hare and Hounds pub in Lothersdale, turn left through a farmyard and on up a track. Soon you are gaining height through fields above the little Stansfield Beck valley, eventually crossing White Hill Lane. Take the concrete track opposite but continue straight on at Hewitts Farm and uphill past Kirk Sykes Farm. The trail now veers generally west onto sandy paths through the heather of Elslack Moor and onwards to the trig pillar on Pinhaw Beacon. At 1273ft (388m) it

Distance:	15¼ miles (25km)
Main Ascents:	Lothersdale to Pinhaw Beacon – 650ft (198m)
Refreshments: (on/near route)	Shop at Thornton-in-Craven; all shops and services at Gargrave; shops, cafes and pubs at Malham. Also pubs at East Marton, Airton and Hanlith/Kirby Malham
Public transport:	Buses from Thornton-in-Craven to Burnley and Skipton (trains from there to Leeds and Manchester); buses from Gargrave to Skipton, Settle (trains to Leeds and Carlisle), also to Malham
Accommodation:	B&Bs at East Marton, Gargrave, Airton, Hanlith, Kirby Malham and Malham; youth hostel at Malham; camping at East Marton, Gargrave and Malham; bunkbarns at Airton and Malham
Maps:	OS Landranger Sheets 103 and 98, OS Explorer Sheet 21 and 10

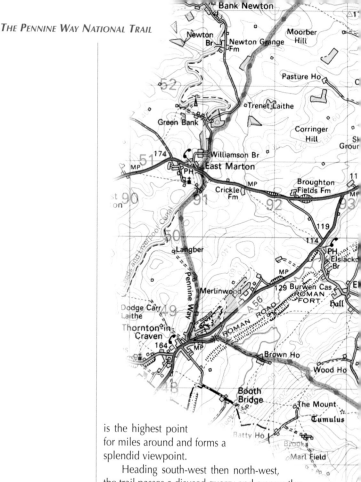

is the highest point
for miles around and forms a
splendid viewpoint.

Heading south-west then north-west,
the trail passes a disused quarry and crosses the
Colne-Carleton road into Clagger Lane leading
towards Elslack village. After about 600m watch for a gate
on the left where the Way leaves the tarmac for a straightforward descent beside a wall. Terrain varies from rough
pasture to marshy pockets, nowhere problematic, until
you reach Brown House farmyard. Beyond the farmhouse
a surfaced lane leads on down, ducks beneath the old
railway and swings up left into Thornton-in-Craven. →

continued on page 70

Head north now along Cam Lane past pretty cottages where the trail continues as a track to the left of Old Cote Farm. Well waymarked, the onward field path climbs then dips to cross Langber Beck, rising over the shoulder of Langber Hill before arriving at the towpath beside the Leeds and Liverpool Canal.

Traffic on the busy A56 apart, Thornton is a pleasant village in a truly rural setting. With the descent from Pinhaw Beacon now behind you, the remainder of this stage encounters no more high ground or sustained gradients.

Measuring a total of 127 miles (203km), this is Britain's longest navigable waterway. During its heyday in the 19th century, it was congested with narrowboats, packet boats and shortboats, all horse-hauled, but the coming of the railways heralded its decline – in common with many other parts of the canal network. By the 1920s waterway transportation had dwindled and the Leeds and Liverpool Canal fell into disuse. However, the modern advent of holiday cruising in narrowboats and other craft has rescued the canal from oblivion so that today it is a well-maintained and popular leisure amenity.

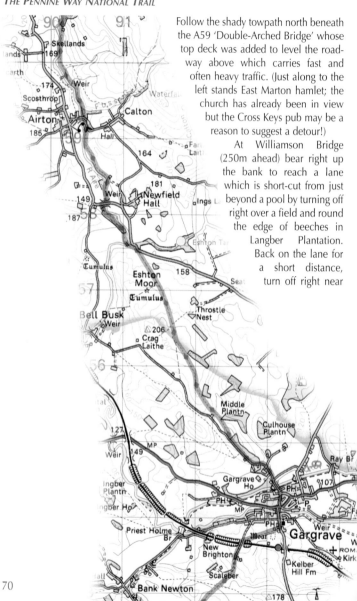

Follow the shady towpath north beneath the A59 'Double-Arched Bridge' whose top deck was added to level the roadway above which carries fast and often heavy traffic. (Just along to the left stands East Marton hamlet; the church has already been in view but the Cross Keys pub may be a reason to suggest a detour!)

At Williamson Bridge (250m ahead) bear right up the bank to reach a lane which is short-cut from just beyond a pool by turning off right over a field and round the edge of beeches in Langber Plantation. Back on the lane for a short distance, turn off right near

The historic double-arched bridge, Leeds and Liverpool Canal

Trenet Laithe ('Laithe' is a common name for barn in this region) and proceed over and down to Crickle Beck; the beck is left then rejoined not far from Newton Grange Farm.

Passing between Moorber and Scaleber hills, fine views open out ahead to the green Aire valley, preceded by Gargrave, now less than a mile away. Losing height gently, you join a concrete lane to cross the Leeds-Carlisle railway line and in 50m turn right over a stile into a cross-field path towards St Andrew's Church and the southern outskirts of Gargrave whose centre lies just over the River Aire.

Once a thriving market town, Gargrave occupies a strategic position in the Aire Gap, an important trans-Pennine communications route. Movement between east and west is facilitated by a temporary lowering of the Pennine hills hereabouts – a feature exploited over many centuries from Roman times through the development of packhorse trade to the building of railways and more recently the channelling of tourist traffic along the A65 into the southern dales. Gargrave is also sizeable enough to offer walkers most of their likely accommodation, shopping, services and refreshment needs – somewhere at which to enjoy a well-earned break from headlong progress before embarking on the final lowland ramble to the enthralling Great Scar Limestone country that awaits.

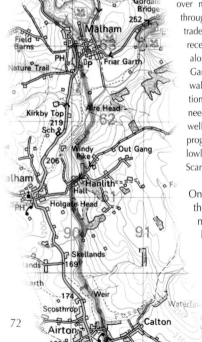

Once over the River Aire and the A65, the trail sets off north past a community hall and a car park and enters a lane crossing the Leeds and Liverpool Canal. In park-like surroundings you skirt round the perimeter of Gargrave House. Just beyond the wood, bear right at a wall stile, following the way-

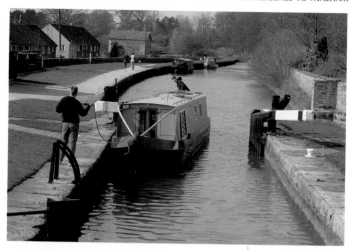

marked field track and paths up over Harrows Hill (the map-marked plantation no longer exists). Soon you enter the Yorkshire Dales National Park and continue down over several fields on the flank of Eshton Moor to join the River Aire. Cross the footbridge to the west bank then cross back again at Newfield Bridge.

Flowery meadows and stretches of tree shade border the Aire whose meanders are shadowed north past the small settlement of Airton on the opposite bank. →

Onward threads the trail through yet more delightful riverside scenery to Hanlith. Here you turn right up the road away from the riverbank and up past Badger House (note the weathervane). Stay on the road until it veers abruptly to the right where the trail leaves through a farmyard on the left, curving round the brow of the valley side to Malham.

As you drop towards Malham, the trail passes above Aire Head, generally accepted as the source of the River Aire. It is an insignificant upwelling of water which has travelled some 2 miles (3km) underground through cracks and channels in the limestone from Water Sinks near Malham Tarn.

Standing by Airton's village green is a 'squatters house' dating from the 1600s when the homeless could apply for permission to build a house on common ground. All around in this area the land has been farmed for thousands of years.

Malham

The natural attractions of Malham Cove, Malham Tarn and Goredale Scar draw in visitors by the thousand. The result is a mixed blessing for Pennine Wayfarers for while there are refreshment places and gift shops in abundance, there is usually a fair crush of humanity to contend with, in the main holiday seasons at least.

The village has a long history and in its earlier days ten or more centuries ago must have seemed a remote spot indeed. Even today the only roads north crawl tentatively over high moorland into the sanctuary of neighbouring dales. As a springboard for walkers, however, there are few more inspiring places in the north of England. Peppered with limestone pavements and 'scars', criss-crossed by ancient trackways and blessed with a carpeting of springy turf, it is little wonder that the Malham area has grown into a veritable honeypot.

OTHER CONNECTING TRAILS

Pendle Way: At Thornton-in-Craven, the Pennine Way comes within ¼ mile (800m) of the 45 mile (72km) Pendle Way. Setting off from the Pendle Heritage Centre, it crosses moorlands and threads river valleys associated with George Fox and the Pendle witches.

Start and Finish: Barrowford, Lancashire (SD 863398)
OS Landranger Sheet: 103
Waymarks: Black Witch logo

Lancashire Trail: This 71 mile (113km) route connects industrial Lancashire with the Pennine Way on a combination of lowland and hill paths.

Start: St Helens, Merseyside (SJ 512956)
Finish: Thornton-in-Craven, North Yorkshire (SD 906484)
OS Landranger Sheets: 102, 103, 108, 109

Leeds and Liverpool Canal: This, the longest single canal in Britain, runs through a wide variety of scenery, from deep countryside to well-known industrial towns. The Pennine Way joins it for a short distance but its total length is 127 miles (203km).

Start: Liverpool Stanley Dock, Merseyside (SJ 343921)
Finish: Leeds city centre, West Yorkshire (SE 293351)
OS Landranger Sheets: 103, 104, 108, 109

STAGE 6
Malham to Horton-in-Ribblesdale

Exploring the scenic wonders of limestone country is a treat in store for Pennine Wayfarers on this stage, even if it does involve a considerable amount of legwork (over 2200ft (670m) of ascent). After a fascinating encounter with Malham Cove and Tarn, the Way climbs the shoulder of Fountains Fell, a more serious hill in both scale and character. After dropping into Silverdale, the second of the day's summits – Pen-y-ghent – rears its shapely profile and provides some airy walking as well as wide panoramas. Thereafter a well-tramped pathway heads downhill to the welcoming village of Horton-in-Ribblesdale. The stage is full of quality hiking but, like some of the higher moorland stretches to the south, needs tackling with an eye to the weather and a supply of food and drink in the rucksack for there are no refreshment points en-route.

The trail leaves Malham heading north along Cove Road; soon after Town Head's group of buildings, including the 17th-century Calamine House, it forks right onto an

Distance:	15 miles (24km)
Main Ascents:	Malham to Malham Tarn – 525ft (160m); Malham Tarn to Fountains Fell – 900ft (275m); Churn Milk Hole to Pen-y-ghent – 800ft (244m)
Refreshments: (on/near route)	Malham and Horton-in-Ribblesdale (the famous Pennine Way Cafe)
Public transport:	Buses from Malham run to Skipton via Gargrave (for trains to Leeds and Manchester); trains from Horton-in-Ribblesdale to Carlisle and Leeds on the Settle-Carlisle line
Accommodation:	B&Bs at Horton-in-Ribblesdale; camping and bunkbarn at Holme Farm, Horton-in-Ribblesdale
Maps:	OS Landranger Sheet 98, OS Explorer Sheet 10

unmistakable pathway which approaches the Cove beside Malham Beck, bordered with ash trees. Before angling away left to climb the stepped path onto the clifftop, it's worth spending a few minutes admiring the extraordinary cove from below, perhaps venturing along the path ahead for a truly worm's-eye view of the huge rock face.

Walkers process towards the base of the curved cliffs of Malham Cove (Photograph by Paddy Dillon)

230ft (70m) high and 650ft (200m) across, the waterfall that once cascaded over the lip above your head was higher than Niagara. Today, little Malham Beck issues from the base, not as one might imagine the continuation of Malham Tarn's outlet that disappears at Water Sinks some distance above. Chemical dye tests in the 1960s established that Malham Tarn's outflow surfaces at Aire Head as we have already seen, so Malham Beck's source lies somewhere deep within the maze of subterranean sumps and passages that honeycomb this area.

After the last Ice Age when the glaciers finally retreated, expanses of Great Scar Limestone were left exposed to the elements. Rainwater containing small amounts of atmospheric carbon dioxide forms a very dilute acid which, over long periods of time, is capable of dissolving limestone. Small grooves and hollows gradually deepened, forming ridges and clefts (the 'clints' and 'grikes' of limestone pavement) and as rain percolated down ever further, it fed underground watercourses which in turn scoured out a complex of cave systems and potholes. Scenery between the Cove and Malham Tarn is typical of glacial 'karst' country: stunted trees, a mixture of lime-loving mountain and lowland flora, and everywhere the bones of the earth pushing through a thin skin of close-cropped turf.

After climbing the steps to clifftop level there is a wonderful panorama from the ankle-twisting limestone pavement over a landscape whose ancient cultivation terraces and enclosure patterns are still discernible today, a thousand years after their formation.

The waymarked trail now continues north-west up the Watlowes dry valley beside a wall, zig-zagging sharp right at the top to skirt Comb Hill in rocky ravines. Eventually you emerge onto flat grassland at Water Sinks. Cross the road ahead (part of the Yorkshire Dales Cycle Way), follow the path to Tarn Foot and enter the Malham Tarn National Nature Reserve, established in 1992. ←

Swinging round the east shore, you converge with Great Close Scar and enter woods past Malham Tarn House.

Now a Field Study Centre owned by the National Trust and managed by the Field Studies Council, the mansion was put up by Lord Ribblesdale on the site of a former shooting lodge. Several well-known literary figures are known to have stayed here when it was a private residence, among them Charles Kingsley whose Water Babies was inspired by the beautiful and then rarely visited scenery.

Follow the onward track, branching off right at a gate just before a house, onto a grassy path. Uphill at first, the trail is guided by drystone walls parallel and not far from the Malham-Arncliffe road which is soon reached. Cross

The existence of Malham Tarn in an area where water disappears below ground is due to the North Craven Fault along which exist beds of Silurian slate which is impervious to water. The lake, extended and stabilised by the addition of a dam at Lord Ribblesdale's instigation in 1791, is a sanctuary for numerous bird and waterfowl species.

continued on
page 81

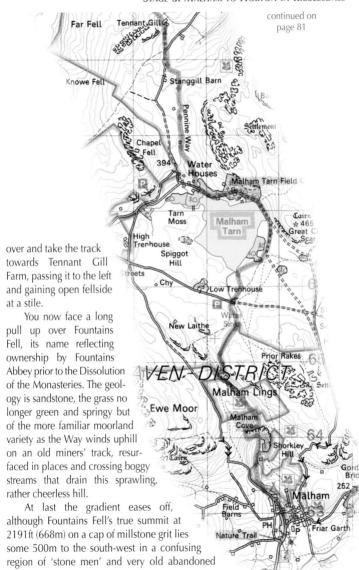

over and take the track towards Tennant Gill Farm, passing it to the left and gaining open fellside at a stile.

You now face a long pull up over Fountains Fell, its name reflecting ownership by Fountains Abbey prior to the Dissolution of the Monasteries. The geology is sandstone, the grass no longer green and springy but of the more familiar moorland variety as the Way winds uphill on an old miners' track, resurfaced in places and crossing boggy streams that drain this sprawling, rather cheerless hill.

At last the gradient eases off, although Fountains Fell's true summit at 2191ft (668m) on a cap of millstone grit lies some 500m to the south-west in a confusing region of 'stone men' and very old abandoned coal pits. Once over a wall stile, the trail dives steeply down a grooved trackway, bearing north-west beside a wall and reaching the Stainforth/Halton Gill road in Silverdale. With Pen-y-ghent well in view, turn left past Rainscar House Farm until just past roadside car parking. Here turn right past Dale Head Farm and on to Churn Milk Hole, a deep crater and pothole indicating that a return has been made to limestone. Swinging north away from the old road to Horton-in-Ribblesdale (a short-cut

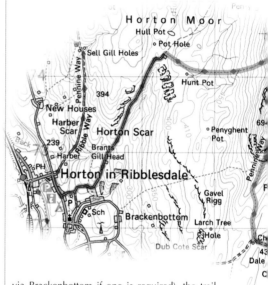

Smallest of Yorkshire's renowned 'Three Peaks', Pen-y-ghent has suffered badly from erosion over the years, in common with the other two, Ingleborough and Whernside. Much work has been carried out to stabilise paths against the onslaught of walkers' boots.

via Brackenbottom if one is required), the trail now approaches the tiered bulk of Pen-y-ghent. Despite its intimidating appearance from this angle, there are no difficulties other than steepness; recent path improvements provide a consolidated line right up to the summit dome at 2277ft (694m) above sea level. The panorama in clear visibility is breathtaking, embracing Pendle Hill, the Bowland Fells, Ingleborough, Whernside, the Howgill Fells and Great Shunner Fell. ←

Cross the wall stile and descend the conspicuous path north-westwards to where it hugs the escarpment.

Now it plunges westwards down the fellside, past Hunt
Pot to reach the upper end of a rough walled lane once
used by packhorse trains. The 300ft (91m) long chasm of
Hull Pot can be visited by making a short detour north;
its waterfall is especially impressive after prolonged wet
weather. Lower down the lane bear right at a fork and
turn right along the B6479 into Horton-in-Ribblesdale.

Horton's old church and the nearby River Ribble may
invite leisurely inspection but probably not before thirst
and appetite have been satisfied. Horton is an obvious
overnight halt and refreshment place between Malham and
Hawes (an otherwise very long and lonely stretch of
rough walking) and the community is well used to welcoming Pennine Wayfarers. Do visit the Pen-y-ghent
Cafe and sign the Pennine Way book, the oldest
one in existence.

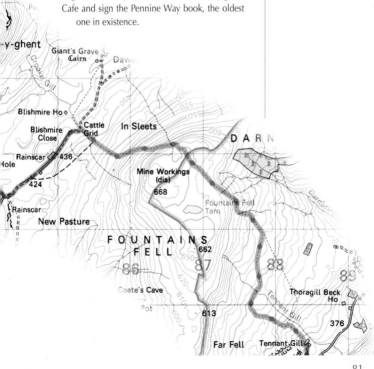

Pen-y-Ghent as seen from near Horton-in-Ribblesdale in the depths of winter (Photograph by Paddy Dillon)

OTHER CONNECTING TRAILS

Crag and Cove Walk: A 20 mile (32km) circuit of dramatic limestone scenery associated with the Mid-Craven Fault.
Start and Finish: Arncliffe, North Yorkshire (SD 932718)
OS Landranger Sheet: 98

Bowland-Dales Traverse: A 95 mile (152km) predominantly upland route over the Forest of Bowland's gritstone hills and the Yorkshire Dales' limestone terraces.
Start: Garstang, Lancashire (SD 492450)
Finish: Richmond, North Yorkshire (NZ 171009)
OS Landranger Sheets: 92, 98, 99, 102, 103

Two Roses Way: A circular route round the hills of the Ribble valley and upper Airedale. 99 miles (158km).
Start and Finish: Whalley, Lancashire (SD 732362)
OS Landranger Sheets: 98, 103

STAGE 7
Horton-in-Ribblesdale to Hawes

Initially in tandem with the Ribble Way, and for a short distance further on with the Dales Way, the Pennine Way itself strikes out across the open moorland of Ribblehead. It is a lonely landscape of wide horizons swelling with the distant silhouettes of higher hills. In poor weather it can seem a bleak passage of walking with few habitations, little in the way of shelter and no refreshment points. Happily the trail is clear on the ground for you are following 'green lanes' or old pack-horse roads for much of the time. These ancient thoroughfares (where they have not been covered by tarmac) provide wonderful pedestrian routes through upland country and are especially characteristic of the Yorkshire Dales. Whatever the weather you are unlikely to lose your way and the 1100ft (340m) of ascent on this stage is achieved without much effort.

Walk north through Horton and from the Crown Inn car park, just by the Ribble road bridge, turn left into Harber Scar Lane, a stony, walled track (the old Settle/Langstrothdale packhorse road) which heads north up Ribblesdale amidst classic Dales scenery of barn-dotted

Distance:	15 miles (24km)
Main Ascents:	Horton-in-Ribblesdale to Kidhow Gate – 1115ft (340m)
Refreshments: (on/near route)	Horton and Hawes; all shops and services at Hawes
Public transport:	Buses from Hawes to Richmond for connections to Darlington (East Coast trains); minibus from Hawes to Garside for trains on Settle-Carlisle line
Accommodation:	B&Bs at Cam Houses, Gayle and Hawes; youth hostel at Hawes; camping and bunkbarn at Cam Houses; campsites at Hawes
Maps:	OS Landranger Sheet 98, OS Explorer Sheet 30

The Pennine way running through the fields to the church at Hawes in winter
(Photograph by Paddy Dillon)

continued on page 86

meadows. You soon come to Sell Gill Holes and Jackdaw Hole.

These pothole entrances, just two among many hereabouts, can be inspected but obviously great care should be exercised in the process. The trail is once again in 'karst' country, the valley once scoured by a south flowing glacier and its limestone left exposed to produce limestone pavements, scars and terraces.

Accompanied by a wall at first, the track rolls on until at a gate you turn off left, climbing over to pass Old Ing Farm not far from the conifers of Greenfield Plantation. Beyond Old Ing the Way resumes its northward course, now on the old walled Settle/ Hawes packhorse road. Winding grassily round Cave Hill and Fair Bottom Hill, it reaches the 200ft (60m) deep limestone ravine of Ling Gill, a National Nature Reserve containing ash, birch, rowan and hazel trees and forming an exciting pathside feature.

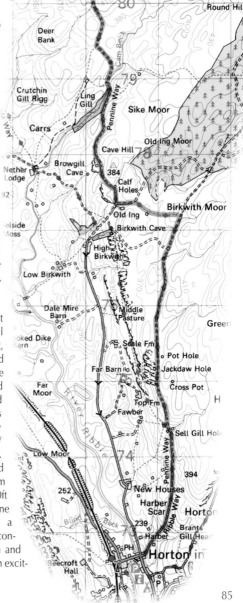

85

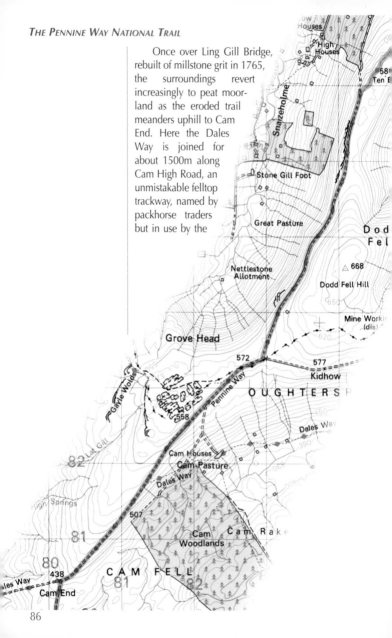

Once over Ling Gill Bridge, rebuilt of millstone grit in 1765, the surroundings revert increasingly to peat moorland as the eroded trail meanders uphill to Cam End. Here the Dales Way is joined for about 1500m along Cam High Road, an unmistakable felltop trackway, named by packhorse traders but in use by the

continued on page 88

Roman military and possibly even those of prehistoric origin.

At a cairned waymark sign the Dales Way forks down right to Cam Houses (accommodation), while the Pennine Way keeps to the high ground. Progress along Cam Fell's moortop road is straightforward if uninspiring, eventually bringing you up to Kidhow Gate at 1877ft (572m) above sea level.

As well as pausing to admire the view (assuming there is one!) which takes in Pen-y-ghent, Ingleborough, Whernside, Wildboar Fell, Buckden Pike and Great Shunner Fell (the trail's next summit), it's worth noting that you are crossing the watershed between the rivers Ribble and Ure.

Although the tarmac road descending to Hawes is only marginally longer, there are no real advantages for walkers since the onward Pennine Way is nowhere difficult and reaches a memorable crescendo as the scenic delights of Wensleydale unfold ahead.

A cairn on Cam High Road marks the junction of the Pennine Way and Dales Way (Photograph by Paddy Dillon)

Forking left off the road onto the old packhorse track (here called West Cam Road) takes you along Dodd Fell's peaty flanks above the deep-set valley of Snaizeholme Beck. Bearing right, there is a gentle height gain at Ten End before the Way, now a grassy path, begins its final descent to Gayle and Hawes. Quite steeply down Rottenstone Hill, it curves right to Gaudy House and enters walled Gaudy Lane to reach a country road. Turn right then immediately left over two fields and left again down to Gayle's West End. Cross over into the lane opposite, down through a modern housing estate, turn left then right along a flagpath above Gayle Beck and follow the path to the right of St Margaret's Church to emerge opposite the White Hart Inn right at the centre of Hawes.

Before leaving Hawes, be sure to visit the Dales Countryside Museum and National Park information centre on the site of the old railway station to the east of the town centre. Here you will gain many fascinating insights into the Pennine landscapes and the lives of its people.

A market town since 1700, Hawes – capital of Wensleydale – makes a welcome staging post on the Pennine Way trek. It is well furnished with shops, services, refreshment places and accommodation and as a bonus is full of character (and characters!). The town serves the local rural communities here in Upper Wensleydale, famed for its cheeses; the hustle and bustle may take time to adjust to after many lonely upland miles on the trail. However, arrival here is auspicious for not only is Hawes itself charming but the Way's next stage to Keld is one of the finest. ←

OTHER CONNECTING TRAILS

Ribble Way: At Horton-in-Ribblesdale the Pennine Way joins the Ribble Way for a short distance to Sell Gill Holes. This 73 mile (116km) trail traces the River Ribble from its mouth at Longton Marsh to its source on Gayle Moor.

Start: Longton, Lancashire (SD 458255)
Finish: Gayle Moor, North Yorkshire (SD 813832)
OS Landranger Sheets: 98, 102, 103
Waymarks: Blue and white 'Ribble Way' wave logo

Dales Way: For a mile on Cam Fell the Pennine Way runs in tandem with this popular 81 mile (130km) trail. It follows scenic dales through the Yorkshire and Howgill fells, crosses the Pennines and descends to the south-eastern part of the Lake District. Three waymarked link routes connect the Dales Way with Leeds, Harrogate and Shipley/Bradford.

Start: Ilkley, West Yorkshire (SE 117476)
Finish: Bowness-on-Windermere, Cumbria (SD 402968)
OS Landranger Sheets: 96, 97, 98, 104
Waymarks: Dales Way signposts within the Yorkshire Dales National Park

Three Peaks Challenge Walk: The famous, classic circuit taking in the summits of Pen-y-ghent, Whernside and Ingleborough. The immensely popular challenge route has suffered badly from erosion, deterring some walkers.

Start and Finish: Horton-in-Ribblesdale, North Yorkshire (SD 809725)
OS Landranger Sheet: 98

Abbott's Hike: Named after its originator, this 107 mile (171km) route links the Dales Way, the Three Peaks Walk and a short section of the Pennine Way to provide an attractive route from Yorkshire to East Lancashire.

Start: Ilkley, West Yorkshire (SE 117476)
Finish: Pooley Bridge, Cumbria (NY 470247)
OS Landranger Sheets: 90, 91, 97, 98, 104

Coast to Coast Trek: A shorter (120 miles (192km)) alternative to Wainwright's classic route. It starts further south and finishes further north, ending on the Cleveland Way from Osmotherley to Saltburn-by-the-Sea. The trail uses good tracks and paths throughout.

Start: Arnside, Cumbria (SD 461788)
Finish: Saltburn-by-the-Sea, North Yorkshire (NZ 668216)
OS Landranger Sheets: 93, 97, 98, 99

STAGE 8
Hawes to Keld

A shortish stage but one that leaves time for exploring Hawes, visiting Hardraw Force, climbing Great Shunner Fell and, in all likelihood, taking refreshment at Thwaite. The walk's axis is a long, ambling traverse over Great Shunner Fell from Wensleydale to Swaledale. Both dales reveal their many charms whatever the weather, though the intervening high ground needs a modicum of luck with visibility to do it justice; in stormy conditions, the less intrepid among us could opt for the moorland road crossing via Butter Tubs pass.

From the east end of Hawes, follow Brunt Acres Road north over the disused railway line, soon cutting a corner across meadows, known as Haylands, on a causey path. Returning to the road, the trail crosses Haylands Bridge, accompanies the River Ure, then strikes off left towards Hardraw on a waymarked flagpath across pastures linked by stiles.

Hardraw is well know for its spectacular 96ft (29m) high waterfall which cascades into a shady limestone gorge situated around a bend about 400m upstream from the bridge. It is England's highest waterfall and well worth

Distance:	12¼ miles (20km)
Main Ascents:	Hardraw to Great Shunner Fell – 1562ft (476m); Thwaite to Kisdon Hill – 492ft (150m)
Refreshments: (on/near route)	Green Dragon pub, Hardraw; the Kearton Restaurant, Thwaite; cafe at Keld
Public transport:	Infrequent buses to Richmond
Accommodation:	B&Bs at Hardraw, Thwaite and Keld; youth hostel at Keld; camping at Hardraw and Keld
Maps:	OS Landranger Sheets 98 and 91, OS Explorer Sheet 30

viewing; a small fee is payable at the Green Dragon pub for use of their private access path.

The Pennine Way continues west from Hardraw bridge for 100m before heading north at a slate-clad house into a stony, walled drove road climbing determinedly up Hollin Hill and veering north-west. Soon you reach the open fell where the vegetation reverts to that of acid moorland. Keep right at the fork on Hearne Top where the trail now trends gradually northward, temporarily blocking off views to the west. To the east across Hearne Beck rises Fossdale Moss crowned by the cairns on Pickersett Edge.

Many Pennine Wayfarers consider the 5 mile (8km) ascent of Great Shunner Fell as a deceptively long one, with several false tops to be surmounted in ever more sombre surroundings lightened only by the call of such

Hardraw Force is well worth a short detour on the way from Hawes to Thwaite (Photograph by Paddy Dillon)

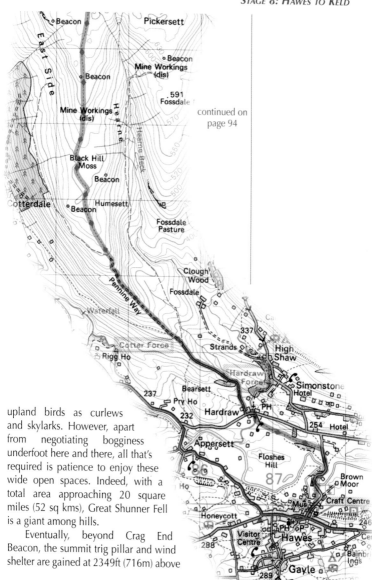

continued on
page 94

upland birds as curlews
and skylarks. However, apart
from negotiating bogginess
underfoot here and there, all that's
required is patience to enjoy these
wide open spaces. Indeed, with a
total area approaching 20 square
miles (52 sq kms), Great Shunner Fell
is a giant among hills.

Eventually, beyond Crag End
Beacon, the summit trig pillar and wind
shelter are gained at 2349ft (716m) above

Despite the proximity of a wire fence, there is a sense of remoteness here: the scale of the land is immense and the feeling of exposure often emphasised by a boisterous wind. If the mist isn't down, there are wonderful views all round, including the now-distant Ingleborough and Pen-y-ghent and, in the west, the wrinkled skyline of the Lake District fells.

sea level, the highest point reached so far on the trek from Edale. ←

Heading off north-east across a fence towards Beacon Cairn, the cairned Way drops steeply then curves round the gathering grounds of Thwaite Beck. Peathags make an unwelcome reappearance but there are flagstones to alleviate otherwise slow going as you lose height and ultimately enter another stony drove road at the intake wall. Flanked by enclosed fields, the trail reaches the road from Kirkby Stephen leading into Thwaite (Norse for 'a woodland clearing').

The old chapel has been converted into flats but of more immediate interest will be the Kearton Restaurant. Few Pennine Wayfarers pass by this opportunity for a well-earned pot of tea (or more!). The restaurant is named after Richard and Cherry Kearton, renowned naturalists in their time

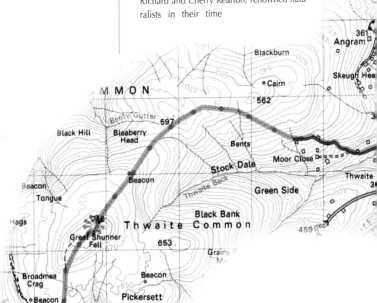

(Cherry was an innovative wildlife photographer) who lived here before moving on to London.

Thus fortified, you now continue by walking east along a side street and from a stile following the field path north-east towards the slopes of Kisdon Hill. There is legwork ahead but marvellous views open up until the meandering route passes Kisdon and attains the shoulder of Kisdon Hill, overlooking the dramatically beautiful valley of the River Swale. For a while you are contouring above high and steep limestone slopes, especially at North Gang Scar, before gently losing height and veering north-west. The clear path is quite stony over scree in places, and can become particularly treacherous in wet weather, but it soon angles downhill through woods opposite Kisdon Force, most prominent of a clutch of waterfalls near the Swale's confluence with East Gill Beck. The onward Pennine Way avoids Keld itself though the hamlet lies a mere 300m ahead and is well geared to accommodating walkers.

Derived from Norse, meaning 'place by the river', Keld nestles in a fold of the moors towards the head of Swaledale. Its higgledy-piggledy cluster of stone cottages might have changed little over the centuries, though today the B6270 does bring in a steady trickle of sightseers during holiday periods.

STAGE 9
Keld to Middleton-in-Teesdale

Although this makes a logical stage in the overall journey, it is also a long one and some walkers may prefer to reduce the day's mileage by detouring to Bowes, or by staying at the youth hostel in Baldersdale or in one of the farms offering accommodation along the way (advance booking advised). Lightweight campers, as always, have a number of options as to their overnight destination.

Between Tan Hill and Baldersdale there is a first taste of wilder North Pennine country as the Yorkshire Dales National Park is left behind. Comparatively little walked, these sprawling, wet moors may seem lonely and remote. Even the presence of the busy A66 road through the Stainmore Gap barely registers as it is quickly crossed, just like Derbyshire's Snake Road before it. Weather and fitness will probably determine whether or not this stage is enjoyable as you celebrate passing the trail's halfway point.

Walk back down to the footbridge over the Swale and bear left up a steep track past East Stonesdale Farm,

Distance:	22 miles (35km)
Main Ascents:	Keld to Tan Hill Inn – 748ft (228m); God's Bridge to Race Yate – 394ft (120m)
Refreshments: (on/near route)	Tan Hill Inn; food shop and pub at Bowes (on Bowes loop); all shops and services at Middleton-in-Teesdale
Public transport:	Buses from Bowes and Middleton-in-Teesdale to Darlington (railway station)
Accommodation:	B&Bs at Tan Hill Inn, Bowes, Baldersdale (limited), Lunedale and Middleton-in-Teesdale; youth hostel at Baldersdale; camping at Tan Hill Inn, Bowes, Lunedale and Middleton-in-Teesdale
Maps:	OS Landranger Sheets 91 and 92, OS Explorer Sheet 30 and 32

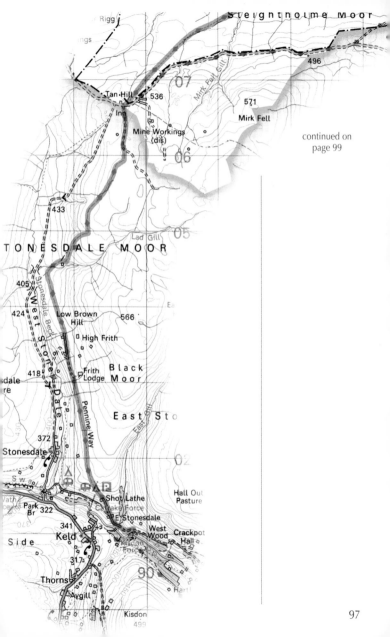

Sleightholme Moor

Rigg

ings

496

Tan Hill 536

Inn

Mine Workings
(dis)

571

Mirk Fell

continued on
page 99

07

06

433

05

STONESDALE MOOR

Lad Gill

405

424

West Stonesdale

Stonesdale Beck

Low Brown
Hill

566

High Frith

418

Frith
Lodge

Black
Moor

B l a c k
M o o r

East Sto

East Gill

Pennine Way

372

Stonesdale

Shot Lathe

Hall Out
Pasture

Park
Br

322

Catrake Force

E Stonesdale

341

Keld

West
Wood

Crackpot
Hall

Kisdon
Force

317

Side

Thorns

Aygill

Kisdon

90

The Tan Hill Inn offers welcome respite from the bleak moors during winter (Photograph by Paddy Dillon)

noting that here the Pennine Way bisects the Northern Coast to Coast route from St Bees in Cumbria to Robin Hood's Bay on Yorkshire's coast, a trail that has mushroomed in popularity over recent years. Keep up right on the old grassy road, perhaps glancing back to Kisdon Hill, the lovely wooded curve of the Swale and Keld on its little green promontory.

When the walls end at Mould Gill you are out over the rough shoulder of Stonesdale Moor, never far from the minor road which runs parallel. Veering north-east more steeply uphill beyond Lad Gill, the cairned track continues over featureless, some might say dreary, moor, pitted with long abandoned colliery shafts dating mainly from the 19th century. Already in view ahead, the Tan Hill Inn draws closer, a capsule of civilisation amidst desolate surroundings. It is the highest pub in England and stands at 1732ft (528m) above sea level.

During the 18th century the inn was at the hub of several packhorse trails; for many years it slaked the thirsts of local coal miners, sheep drovers and other tradespeople who travelled over these moors. The inn is also situated at the convergence of present-day motor roads and on

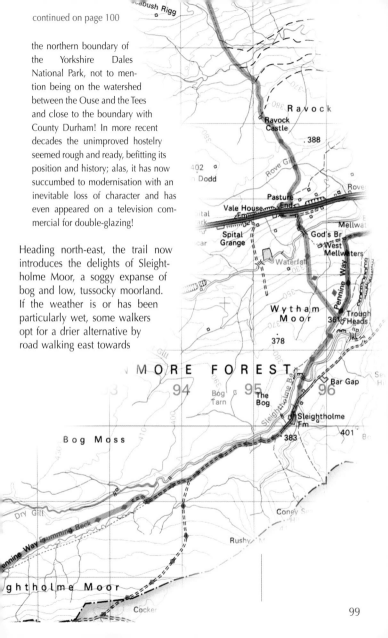

continued on page 100

the northern boundary of the Yorkshire Dales National Park, not to mention being on the watershed between the Ouse and the Tees and close to the boundary with County Durham! In more recent decades the unimproved hostelry seemed rough and ready, befitting its position and history; alas, it has now succumbed to modernisation with an inevitable loss of character and has even appeared on a television commercial for double-glazing!

Heading north-east, the trail now introduces the delights of Sleightholme Moor, a soggy expanse of bog and low, tussocky moorland. If the weather is or has been particularly wet, some walkers opt for a drier alternative by road walking east towards

99

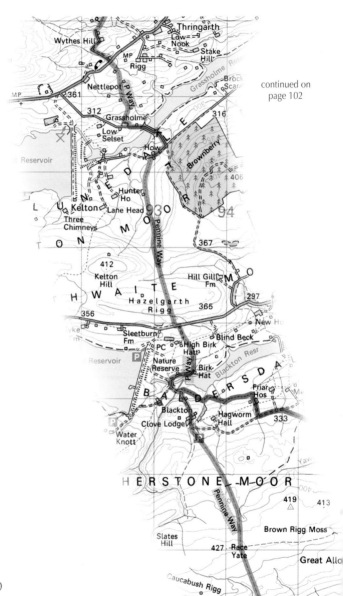

continued on
page 102

Thringarth
Wythes Hill
Low
Nook
Stake
Hill
MP
Rigg
Grassholme Resr
Brock
Scar
Nettlepot
361
312
Grassholme
316
Low
Selset
How
Brownberry
406
Hunter
Ho
Kelton
Lane Head
930
Three
Chimneys
367
412
Kelton
Hill
Hill Gill
Fm
M
297
Hazelgarth
Rigg
365
356
New Ho
Sleetburn
Fm
Blind Beck
PC
High Birk
Hatt
Blackton Resr
Nature
Reserve
Birk
Hat
Friar
Hos
Blackton
Hagworm
Hall
333
Clove Lodge
Water
Knott

HERSTONE MOOR

419
413
Slates
Hill
Brown Rigg Moss
427
Race
Yate
Great Allo
Caucabush Rigg

100

Arkengarthdale for about 2 miles (3km) then forking north-east at Great Cocker to follow the Sleightholme Moor Road track which rejoins the main route beyond the boggy ground.

The main path however stays along the firmer north bank of Frumming Beck, avoiding much of the wetter going to the south which gave Sleightholme Moor such a bad name among wayfarers in the past. Converging with a shooters' track (this is grouse moorland) you cross Frumming Beck and soon reach a farm lane which becomes metalled and passes Sleightholme Farm in its green hollow. In about 300m the Way forks left off the road, crosses Sleightholme Beck on Intake Bridge and continues on to Trough Heads. Here the main route and the so-called 'Bowes Loop' part company, the latter summarised when the main route reaches Clove Lodge Farm above Baldersdale.

God's Bridge is a natural slab of limestone spanning the infant River Greta (Photograph by Paddy Dillon)

Fork left (north-west) at Trough Heads Farm over heathery moorland to a wall and a northward shift descending to cross the River Greta at God's Bridge, an ancient crossing point.

> The river itself vanishes beneath massive limestone slabs (limestone intrudes here into the gritstone of Stainmore). Except in times of flood only a deep pool underneath the bridge is visible, the water making a subterranean journey.

Beyond an old limekiln the trail cuts through the dismantled railway line's embankment and passes through a tunnel beneath the frenetic A66 trunk road at Pasture End. The next few miles of empty heather and rough grasses possess few redeeming features yet even here if conditions are reasonable, inspiration may be drawn from the fresh breezes and the play of cloud shadows. There may be some excitement too at the prospect of approaching the Way's halfway point.

Keeping generally west of north, the trail first meanders over Ravock Moor then descends to the footbridge spanning Deepdale Beck. In company with a wall it then rises to the crest of Race Yate at 1402ft (427m) and in the same direction continues over featureless Cotherstone Moor before dropping to a corner of the road near Clove Lodge farm, with Baldersdale's reservoirs now in sight.

THE BOWES LOOP

There are plans to construct a bridge over the River Greta and thus allevite the difficulties in crossing the stepping stones between Lady Myres and Swinholme farms when the river is in spate. Until this is built, it would be wise to use the road via Gilmonby or arrange accommodation further along the main route. For those wishing to visit Bowes, the following summary can be used in conjunction with a map.

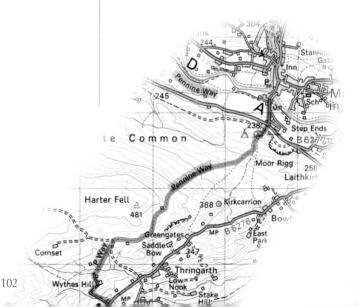

The old Grassholme Bridge appears when Grassholme reservoir is low (Photograph by Paddy Dillon)

From Trough Heads press on north-east on the path linking the farmsteads of East Mellwaters, West Charity and Lady Myres. Either cross the River Greta to Swinholme and continue to Bowes or carry straight on along the farm track past West Pasture to Gilmonby and thence to Bowes.

→ This alternative loop leaves Bowes' west end by a lane crossing the A66 dual carriageway, continuing along it to cross Tute Hill with its wartime military associations still evident. From Levy Pool you cross Deepdale Beck in rather desolate, undulating surroundings and beyond some boggy terrain around Hazelgill Beck traverse the shoulder of Kearton Rigg to the remarkable gritstone outcrop of Goldsborough, a landmark for miles around on the anonymous moors. Five hundred metres ahead the Bowes Loop enters a moor road; either this or the field path via East Friar House Farm to Blackton Bridge re-unite you with the main Pennine Way.

Cross Blackton Bridge between Baldershead and Blackton reservoirs and swing right to Birk Hatt Farm, erstwhile home of Hannah Hauxwell. From here you strike north on a gravel path past High Birk Hatt Farm to reach a lane leading up from Hury to Balder Head. (This is the trail's halfway mark.)

Turn left then in 50m right onto the unkempt slopes of Hazelgarth Rigg, part of Mickleton Moor. Soon you

As well as having the usual amenities of a large village, Bowes has a prominent castle ruin set on the site of a Roman fort here in the strategically important Stainmore Gap. In 1832 Charles Dickens came to Teesdale to research material for his novel Nicholas Nickleby, much of which is based on what he found at Bowes.

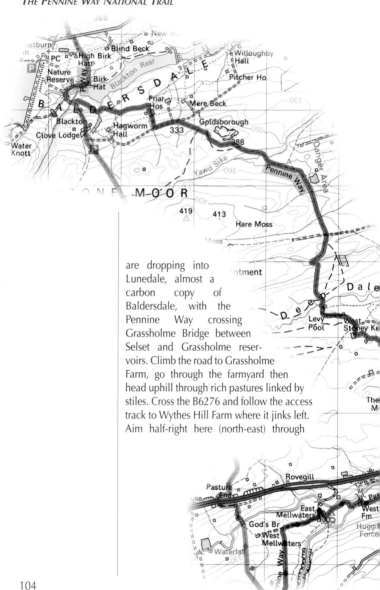

are dropping into Lunedale, almost a carbon copy of Baldersdale, with the Pennine Way crossing Grassholme Bridge between Selset and Grassholme reservoirs. Climb the road to Grassholme Farm, go through the farmyard then head uphill through rich pastures linked by stiles. Cross the B6276 and follow the access track to Wythes Hill Farm where it jinks left. Aim half-right here (north-east) through another succession of small enclosed fields round the flanks of Harter Fell.

Over to your right rises the plantation-crowned hill called Kirkcarrion, site of a large ancient tumulus. It is conspicuous over long distances in this region, from Tan Hill to Langdon Beck in Teesdale.

Well waymarked, the trail descends towards the patchwork fields and welcome habitations of Middleton-in-Teesdale. Below, through a gate, you reach the B6277 which takes you over the River Tees on County Bridge, providing access to fleshpots of this capital of Upper Teesdale.

Lead mining flourished here during the 19th century, boosting the local economy and population. By 1815 Middleton had already become the headquarters of the Quaker-owned London Lead Company whose philanthropy cared well for its workforce and developed the town, leaving a fascinating architectural legacy. (Durham County Council publish a 'Walkabout' booklet describing a town trail taking in all the main features.) On 12th May 1868 the Tees Valley Railway reached Middleton, further enhancing its position as a social and economic centre for the region. It remains thus to this day, largely unspoiled by tourism attractions, a down-to-earth, authentic, slightly old-fashioned dales town. To Pennine Wayfarers arriving from the wastes of Sleightholme Moor and the like, Middleton can seem like nirvana – a chance to replenish supplies, re-charge batteries and enjoy the proximity of fellow human beings!

An ornate cast-iron drinking fountain in the middle of Middleton-in-Teesdale (Photograph by Paddy Dillon)

Pine trees on Kirkcarrion form a notable landmark above Middleton-in-Teesdale (Photograph by Paddy Dillon)

From Middleton to Dufton the Pennine Way runs in tandem with the Teesdale Way, a long-distance trek of more recent date that traces the River Tees west to east from its source under Cross Fell to the Teesmouth estuary, a distance of 100 miles (160km). Downstream from Middleton there is much to explore as the river leaves behind its upland birthplace and meanders, ever broader, past beautiful woodland, pretty villages, historical sites and wetlands down to its meeting with the North Sea.

OTHER CONNECTING TRAILS

The Northern Coast to Coast Walk: Near Keld the Pennine Way intersects this 190 mile (304km) trail which Wainwright pioneered in 1972 and which has since enjoyed growing popularity. It links the Irish and North seas and takes in three National Parks. Although individual variations are made, the trail is essentially high level in character, crossing the Lake District fells, the Pennines and the North York Moors.
Start: St Bees, Cumbria (NX 959119)
Finish: Robin Hood's Bay, North Yorkshire (NZ 953048)
OS Landranger Sheets: 89, 90, 91, 92, 93, 94, 98, 99, 100

STAGE 10
Middleton-in-Teesdale to Dufton

This long stage is often divided into two in order to allow longer in Middleton and to savour Teesdale at a leisurely pace. However, further up the dale accommodation is limited, Langdon Beck being the last place at which to overnight unless you are camping.

Of all the Pennine Way's stages this is perhaps the most special. Pastoral riverside scenery through flowery meadows leads past bridges and the famous waterfalls of Low and High Force before the trail breaks out into wilder country, characterised by cliffs of Whin Sill dolerite. Beyond dramatic Cauldron Snout there is a crossing of the watershed to High Cup Nick, the stage's sensational finale, followed by a straightforward descent to Dufton. As with all the trail's higher stretches, try to obtain a weather forecast and ensure you are properly equipped.

A combination of track and path lead the Pennine Way from a point about 100m south of Middleton's County Bridge (until 1974 the Tees formed the boundary between Yorkshire and Durham). For 3 miles (5km) or so the River Tees swings in great lazy loops on the shallow

Distance:	21 miles (34km)
Main Ascents:	Holwick Head Bridge to Rasp Hill on Dufton Fell – 1050ft (320m)
Refreshments: (on/near route)	Meals, snacks, drinks at Langdon Beck Hotel; food shop and pub at Dufton
Public transport:	Infrequent buses from Dufton to Appleby for trains on the Settle/Carlisle line
Accommodation:	B&Bs at Forest-in-Teesdale; Langdon Beck Hotel and Dufton; youth hostels at Langdon Beck and Dufton; camping/bunkbarn at Holwick and Dufton
Maps:	OS Landranger Sheet 91, OS Explorer Sheet 31

gradient, short-cut by the path which passes stands of oak, ash and alder.

continued on
page 111

This is indeed a section of rare geological and botanical delights. You might spot 'kettles' in the flat riverbed shales once the path regains the riverbank, itself approaching Scoberry Bridge. These circular hollows have been scoured by hard pebbles moved in the swirling water. Up to the left, Holwick Lodge is backed by the Whin Sill crags of Holwick Scars.

The original Wynch Bridge, built in 1704 by local lead miners, was possibly Europe's first suspension bridge. Unfortunately it collapsed in 1820 while 11 people were crossing and one man was drowned. The present bridge dates from 1830.

About ¼ mile (800m) beyond Scoberry Bridge you reach Wynch Bridge, giving access across the Alston road to Bowlees Visitor Centre near the village of Newbiggin-in-Teesdale; if time allows, it's well worth visiting. ←

Just upstream lies Low Force where the Tees' peaty waters cascade between low walls of whinstone – a pleasant spot at which to linger.

The word 'force' (pronounced 'foss' locally) derives from the old Norse 'fors' used by Scandinavian settlers a thousand years ago.

Low Force is passed near Bowlees on the way upstream beside the River Tees (Photograph by Paddy Dillon)

A mile of walking through riverside meadows linked by step-through stiles brings you to Holwick Head Bridge where the trail mounts steps to continue at a slightly higher level above the narrowing river channel. Before long, its thunder perhaps already announcing its presence, you are confronted by High Force, probably Teesdale's best known scenic attraction. (Non-walkers can reach it along the north bank by payment of a toll at the roadside hotel.)

This is England's largest (but not its highest) waterfall, with a drop

The Tees plunges 70ft (21m) at High Force

of 69ft (21m). Its existence is due to the Whin Sill whose dark, crystalline dolerite, locally called whinstone, has resisted erosion. Very gradually the waterfall has retreated to form its dramatic gorge. Care should be taken if scrambling around above the falls, as despite the 'taming' effect of Cow Green Reservoir upstream, unpredictable water surges can occur after heavy rain.

The well-constructed path leads onward past Force Garth Quarry whose roadstone extraction incongruously causes noise and considerable dust pollution. Crossing two streams the trail rises

continued on page 113

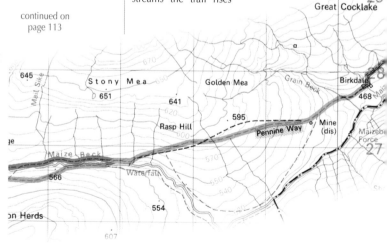

through an extraordinary tangle of gnarled juniper bushes on Bracken Rigg. Rough pastureland and a succession of white-painted stiles, and stretches of made path, follow until at High Crag you drop more steeply through a rocky depression and walk up round to the left of Cronkley Farm. Go down the track and over the river bridge, now on the north bank of Harwood Beck, a major tributary of the Tees which it joins here.

There are thrilling views ahead to a skyline of high moors yet to be encountered as you follow the flowery, sometimes stony meadow path opposite Wheysike House and arrive at Sayer Hill Bridge.

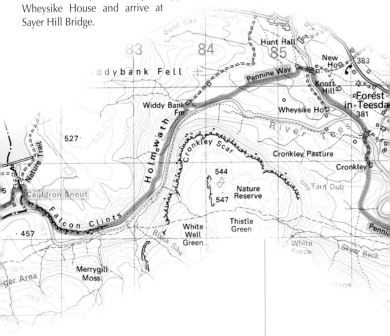

The many whitewashed farms and cottages in Upper Teesdale belong to Lord Barnard's Raby Estate. The whitewashing tradition dates back to when a member of the then Duke of Cleveland's family was lost in a storm; unable to find shelter he narrowly escaped death. The

Duke decreed that from that day on, all tenanted farmsteads on his estate be painted white to show up clearly to a traveller in need.

Note: Walkers wishing to stay at Langdon Beck youth hostel or at Forest-in-Teesdale should take the farm lane up to the right which meets the B6277 almost opposite the hostel, with the village just along to the right. To reach the Langdon Beck Hotel continue along the west bank of Harwood Beck to the Cow Green road at a ford; turn right to the junction with the B6277 where the hotel is situated.

The Pennine Way now crosses Sayer Hill Bridge, climbs past

Wheysike House is seen across Langdon Beck in Upper Teesdale (Photograph by Paddy Dillon)

Sayer Hill Farm and heads west over rough pasture linked by white-painted stiles, crossing two small stream valleys in the process. Turning left onto the track brings you to the isolated farmstead of Widdybank, now an office for English Nature. Easy, spacious walking along Holmwath opposite the Whin Sill crags of Cronkley Scar precedes a narrowing of the valley and before long you are clambering over awkward boulders, cheek by jowl with the clattering Tees at the foot of Falcon

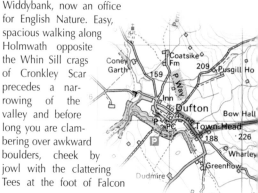

Clints' 100ft (30m) cliffs. After a brief respite there is another ankle-twisting stretch to negotiate until a slight opening out at river level announces arrival at Cauldron Snout. This 220ft (60m) cascade is a stirring sight and the trail scrambles up rocky ledges right beside the thrashing torrent to emerge below Cow Green Reservoir dam.

The Tees' waterfalls (as well as High Cup Nick and the Hadrian's Wall crags ahead) are all formed by the Whin Sill, a great seam of igneous dolerite running for almost 90 miles (300km) across northern Britain. Meanwhile, unseen behind its dam from this angle, Cow Green Reservoir gathers its water from some 20 square miles (52 sq kms) of moorland, regulating the flow downstream so as to provide a consistent supply, especially to the industrial complexes around Middlesbrough and Teesside. Indeed it was largely for their benefit that the reservoir was built in the late 1960s, despite vehement opposition from conservationists.

The large Upper Teesdale National Nature Reserve, and Widdybank Fell in particular, is a last refuge for certain arctic flora surviving from the last Ice Age. Many plants hereabouts are unique in Western Europe, due in part to the existence of

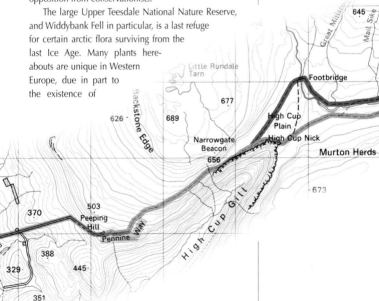

Below Cow Green the Tees thunders down Cauldron Snout

lime-rich 'sugar limestone' but also to the extended and often severe winters which allow meadow species to cast their seeds before haymaking starts. Long sections of boardwalk and flagstones have been installed to protect the flora from trampling.

Cross the bridge below the dam, thus walking from County Durham into Cumbria, and follow the access track to Birkdale farmhouse, slipping past unobtrusively. It is hard to imagine a more remote habitation! After crossing the Grain Beck footbridge the trail begins to climb on a reconstructed path. Little remains of Moss Shop, 19th-century lead miners' living quarters and workshop. Further on there are intermittent stretches of flagstones as you gain the crest of Rasp Hill on the vast flanks of Dufton Fell. These days, even in mist, it would be hard to lose the way and the going is much more straightforward than it once was on this boggy moorside.

Signs to the south warn of a military firing range, part of the Warcop Training Range which encompasses much of lofty Murton Fell and excludes walkers.

About ¼ mile (800m) past the point where the trail meets Maize Beck (another major tributary of the Tees), a tall cairn marks the usual crossing where the beck is broad, shallow and stony. However, in times of spate it is a different proposition and then you can simply stay along the north bank until you reach a footbridge at a spectacular little gorge: this is the so-called 'Flood Route'. In mist you may need to consult your map and compass to confirm the onward south-westerly course from the bridge to High Cup Nick. (The stepping stones recently installed over Maize Beck were destroyed by a storm in August 2002. The river bed itself is now wider and at the time of writing the Countryside Agency is considering how best to solve the crossing problem. It may be necessary to construct a bridge).

Having negotiated Maize Beck, the ordinary route shadows its south bank with wide views north towards the Tees' headwaters below Cross Fell. Ahead the trail curves away from Maize Beck, gradually heading southwest over a rather featureless upland landscape. But a surprise awaits you! Arrival at High Cup Nick from the east must rank as one of the country's most astonishing scenic revelations. Indeed many consider it to be the North Pennines' 'tour de force' and it is to be hoped that you enjoy good conditions for it. →

Keeping to the right hand (northern) edge, the trail rises gently, passing above Nichol's Chair, a slender rock pinnacle named after a Dufton cobbler reputed to have soled and heeled a pair of boots while sitting on top! Beyond a clear spring – Hannah's Well – the path becomes a rocky ledge as it approaches Narrowgate. Then, well cairned, it curves round the flanks of Peeping Hill, eventually entering a walled track which hastens towards Dufton, passing Bow Hall. At the road (Town Head) turn right and walk along to Dufton's centre.

With its complement of youth hostel, pub (The Stag Inn) and general store/post office, the village is a welcome stopover for Pennine wayfarers. Red sandstone houses line the shady green, the fountain having been installed by the same 'Quaker Company' responsible for much of Middleton-in-Teesdale's development during the 19th-century heyday of lead mining.

Not only is there a bird's-eye view down the classic 'U' shaped, glaciated valley of High Cup Gill, but ranged along the western horizon beyond the Vale of Eden lie the corrugated silhouettes of Lakeland's fells. High Cup's rim is, once again, formed from the Whin Sill, here seen as a ruler-straight lip of columnar basalt.

High Cup Nick

OTHER CONNECTING TRAILS

Teesdale Way: From Middleton-in-Teesdale over to Dufton, the Pennine Way runs in tandem with the 100 mile (162km) Teesdale Way. The trail is usually walked west to east, tracing the course of the River Tees from Cauldron Snout (nearest available access to its source) down to Teesmouth where it enters the North Sea. This varied trail threads through dales countryside, woodland, rolling farmland, wetlands and ends with a passage through the industrial heartland of Teesside.

Start: Dufton, Cumbria (NY 690251)

Finish: South Gare Breakwater, Teesmouth, Cleveland (NZ 557284)

OS Landranger Sheets: 91, 92, 93

Waymarks: Follows Pennine Way to Middleton-in-Teesdale; dipper logo in County Durham and salmon logo in Cleveland.

North Pennine Path: A 110 mile (176km) circuit designed as a tour of youth hostels at Langdon Beck, Dufton, Ninebanks and Edmunbyers. The trail traverses remote uplands and also includes Weardale, Teesdale, the Eden Valley, South Tynedale, the Allendales and Derwentside.

Start and Finish: Stanhope Station, County Durham (NY 998387)

OS Landranger Sheets: 187, 91, 92

STAGE 11
Dufton to Alston

On reaching Dufton you are further from Kirk Yetholm than when you set out from Middleton-in-Teesdale! However, most Pennine Wayfarers will consider this westerly 'detour' perfectly acceptable. Even if there were rights-of-way across the indeterminate, bog-ridden expanse of Dufton Fell, few would choose such an arduous alternative in preference to enjoying High Cup and taking advantage of Dufton's amenities.

Dufton to Alston undoubtedly represents a hard day's hike but it could be shortened by halting at Garrigill. Either way, the reward for your efforts is a traverse of the Pennines' highest summit. The stage begins with a fairly sustained ascent to Knock Fell followed by ups and downs over the two Dun Fells. Then comes Cross Fell where compass navigation might be necessary in mist, although once down on the northern side a broad track delivers you straightforwardly to Garrigill and the valley of the River South Tyne. Needless to say, loins should be girded up and adequate energy food and drink carried as there are no refreshments and very little shelter until near the end of the stage.

Distance:	20 miles (32km)
Main Ascents:	Dufton to Knock Fell – 2080ft (634m); Dunfell Hush to Great Dun Fell – 259ft (90m); Tees Head to Cross Fell – 404ft (123m)
Refreshments: (on/near route)	Food shop, teas and pub at Garrigill all shops and services at Alston
Public transport:	Infrequent buses from Garrigill to Alston
Accommodation:	B&Bs at Garrigill and Alston; youth hostel at Alston; camping at Alston
Maps:	OS Landranger Sheets 91 and 86, OS Explorer Sheet 31

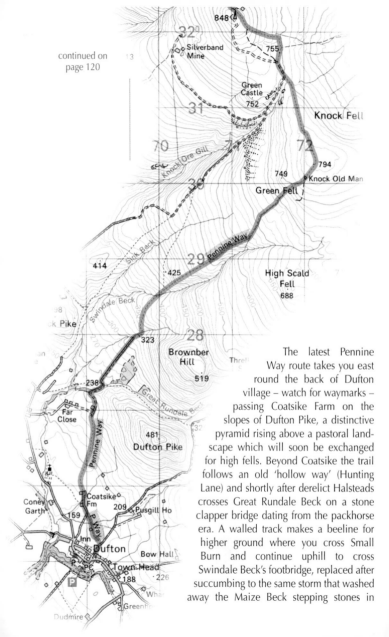

continued on
page 120

848

32

Silverband
Mine

755

Green
Castle
752

31

Knock Fell

70

72

Knock (Ore Gill)

794

749

Knock Old Man

30

Green Fell

Pennine Way

414

Sink Beck

29

425

High Scald
Fell
688

Swindale Beck

Pike

28

323

Brownber
Hill

519

Threl

238

Great Rundale B

Far
Close

Pennine Way

481

Dufton Pike

Coney
Garth

Coatsike
Fm

209

Pusgill Ho

159

P Way

Inn

Dufton

Bow Hall

P
PC

Town-Head

188

226

P

Wha

Greenh

Dudmire

The latest Pennine
Way route takes you east
round the back of Dufton
village – watch for waymarks –
passing Coatsike Farm on the
slopes of Dufton Pike, a distinctive
pyramid rising above a pastoral landscape which will soon be exchanged
for high fells. Beyond Coatsike the trail
follows an old 'hollow way' (Hunting
Lane) and shortly after derelict Halsteads
crosses Great Rundale Beck on a stone
clapper bridge dating from the packhorse
era. A walled track makes a beeline for
higher ground where you cross Small
Burn and continue uphill to cross
Swindale Beck's footbridge, replaced after
succumbing to the same storm that washed
away the Maize Beck stepping stones in

Dufton's village green and Dufton Pike

August 2002. Climbing becomes steeper now, still in a north-easterly direction and marked by occasional cairns.

> The path lies alongside Knock Hush, a scar on the hillside made by 19th-century lead mining. In order to expose mineral ore lying beneath the surface, miners would build a temporary dam at the top of a slope. When accumulated water was released it scoured away the vegetation and revealed the subsoil for inspection.

Eventually you top out at Knock Old Man, an impressive cairn, and shortly after reach the summit of Knock Fell, at 2604ft (794m) the highest ground reached so far on the northerly trek. A mile of simple walking past long-abandoned mine workings and natural hollows leads to the tarmac road servicing the conspicuous radar station atop Great Dun Fell. Do not take the road however

Knock Old Man

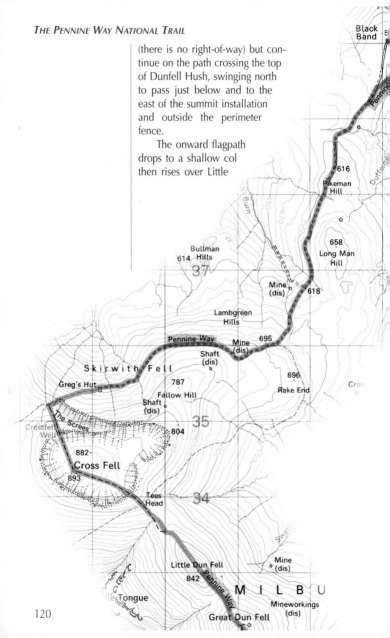

(there is no right-of-way) but continue on the path crossing the top of Dunfell Hush, swinging north to pass just below and to the east of the summit installation and outside the perimeter fence.

The onward flagpath drops to a shallow col then rises over Little

Black Band

Pennine

616
Pikeman Hill

Dunfell

658
Long Man Hill

Mine (dis)
618

Bullman Hills
614

37

Lambgreen Hills

Burn

Pennine Way
Mine (dis)
695

Shaft (dis)

Skirwith Fell

696
Rake End

Greg's Hut

787
Fallow Hill

Shaft (dis)

35

The Screes

Crossfell Well

804

882
Cross Fell

893

Tees Head

34

Swat

Mine (dis)

Little Dun Fell

842

Pennine Way

M I L B U

Tongue

Mineworkings (dis)

Great Dun Fell

continued on page 123

Dun Fell (2763ft (842m)) before descending to Tees Head.

The flag path over bog at Tees Head

Before the installation of flagstones, this was a notoriously spongy section. To the east the infant Tees twists and turns, forming miniature waterfalls and soon growing to a sizeable beck but there is no public right of access beside it. This remote and inhospitable region of the Pennines, its bog and heather almost devoid of paths and habitations, holds much of botanical value and is protected by the 10,000 acre (4000 hectare) Moor House Nature Reserve.

Threading up through Cross Fell's rim of scree and heading west-north-west across the grassy, stony plateau brings you to the summit windbreak and trig pillar at 2930ft (893m) above sea level.

This is England's loftiest point outside the Lake District and views are excellent if the weather smiles. However, weather will be the making or marring of your Cross Fell encounter. Its high profile, thrusting into the airstreams crossing Britain, often produces cloud and wind, adding considerably to the fell's forbidding bleakness. The famous Helm Wind, caused by air rising from the east, cooling over the summit and accelerating down into the valleys just west of the fell, can cause damaging gusts.

Leave the summit in a direction a little west of north, descending through the screes near Crossfell Well and reaching a prominent track. Turn right, soon reaching a bothy called Greg's Hut. →

Greg's Hut, an old mine building, was rebuilt by the Mountain Bothies Association in memory of John Gregory who was killed by an avalanche in the Alps in 1968. The hut is basic but well maintained and offers virtually the only shelter on this rugged section of trail.

Continue along the track on Blackstone Edge with a vast panorama north over the gathering grounds of the South Tyne.

Although not substantiated, one theory suggest that this track may have been an old corpse road between Garrigill and Kirkland in days when consecrated ground was not available in the upper South Tyne valley. No doubt it was welcomed by the 18th and 19th-century lead miners as a convenient thoroughfare to their productive workings here deep in the hills. Spoil heaps and the entrances to various mine levels are in evidence all around, as are lovely pale blue and mauve fragments of fluorspar.

Along the flanks of Long Man and Pikeman hills the trail edges slowly downhill. An official short-cut across a corner of walled track is rarely used and a steeper stretch of descent from Black Band quickly leads down to the minor valley road at Garrigill.

An unassuming hamlet with a pleasant, shady green at its centre, Garrigill offers a welcome to Pennine Wayfarers in the form of a pub (the George and Dragon), a post office and several bed and breakfast places.

Contrasting sharply with the rugged fells just negotiated,

A splendid and solid Pennine farmhouse passed on the way to Alston (Photograph by Paddy Dillon)

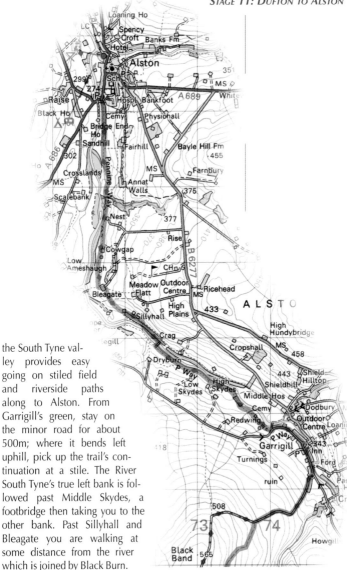

the South Tyne val-
ley provides easy
going on stiled field
and riverside paths
along to Alston. From
Garrigill's green, stay on
the minor road for about
500m; where it bends left
uphill, pick up the trail's continuation at a stile. The River
South Tyne's true left bank is followed past Middle Skydes, a
footbridge then taking you to the
other bank. Past Sillyhall and
Bleagate you are walking at
some distance from the river
which is joined by Black Burn.

123

Alston's claim to being England's highest market town is challenged by Derbyshire's Buxton which occupies a similar elevation. However there any similarity ends, for Alston is quite unique; its picturesque grey and white buildings rise to a steepled hilltop church. During its formative years as a lead miners' town, Alston would have been less aesthetically pleasing by far. With the advent of modern-day tourism its functional architecture has been somewhat re-vamped and an element of 'chic' introduced into its shops, though vestiges of more traditional retailing can still be found. Alston has been put on the tourist map largely by the development of the preserved South Tynedale Railway. Nevertheless rucksacks can be replenished and the inner man satisfied in preparation for the next leg up the South Tyne valley to Hadrian's Wall.

Not far beyond Low Nest the trail enters a popular wall-lined track, finally emerging near the youth hostel at the A686 road. Alston town centre lies straight ahead and up to the right, though the onward Pennine Way crosses the road bridge to pursue its close association with the South Tyne.

OTHE CONNECTING TRAILS

Alternative Pennine Way: On Dufton Fell and further ahead at several more points, the Pennine Way meets its Alternative, created both to relieve pressure on the National Trail itself and to provide a more scenically varied route. It does however involve more climbing as it crosses high ground rather than staying on the tops. The total length is 268 miles (429km).
Start: Ashbourne, Derbyshire (SK 178469)
Finish: Jedburgh, Scottish Borders (NT 651204)
OS Landranger Sheets: 74, 80, 87, 91, 98, 99, 104, 110, 119

Helm Wind Challenge Walk: A circuit of Cross Fell from the north
Start and Finish: Garrigill, Cumbria (NY 744417)
OS Landranger Sheets: 87, 91

Alternative Coast to Coast: A 193 mile (309km) walk joining Walney Island near Barrow-in-Furness with Holy Island on the east coast. Several Lakeland peaks are climbed and several delightful Lakeland villages are visited and the full length of Ullswater is walked. Between Penrith and Hexham the route crosses the Northern Pennines and crosses the Pennine Way at Alston. It then crosses the Cheviot Hills.
Start: Walney Island
Finish: Holy Island
OS Landranger Sheets: 96, 90, 91, 86, 87, 80, 81, 75

STAGE 12
Alston to Greenhead

As A.W. Wainwright rightly points out in his original
Pennine Way Companion, the logical continuation of the
trail from Cross Fell is northward along the main watershed, crossing Cold Fell to the Carlisle-Newcastle gap
where the Pennine range itself ends. However, this
would have posed logistical problems for the majority of
walkers, not to mention greatly increasing the arduous-
ness of the terrain involved. Instead we have a route
which features Hadrian's Wall, Wark Forest and the
Cheviot Hills, offering considerably more scenic diversi-
ty than a true 'Pennine Way' would have done.

That said, the stretch linking Alston with the Roman
wall is not a scintillating one, though the prospect of
what lies immediately ahead is usually sufficient a spur
to keep the spirits high. Whilst it is not a physically
demanding walk, it is fairly convoluted in places requir-
ing a frequent eye on the map and waymarks.

Set off from Alston's southern end, cross the River South
Tyne bridge and turn right along the A689 Slaggyford
road, one that is encountered quite often during the
hike up the valley. Almost immediately a waymark sign
indicates the trail's continuation as a track parallel to the

Distance:	18 miles (29km)
Main Ascents:	Lambley to Wain Rigg – 295ft (90m)
Refreshments: (on/near route)	Pubs at Slaggyford and Greenhead
Public transport:	Buses from Alston to Haltwhistle via Slaggyford; buses from Greenhead to Carlisle and Newcastle; trains from Haltwhistle to Carlisle and Newcastle
Accommodation:	B&Bs at Slaggyford and Greenhead; youth hostel at Greenhead; camping and bunkhouse at Greenhead
Maps:	OS Landranger Sheet 86, OS Explorer Sheet 43

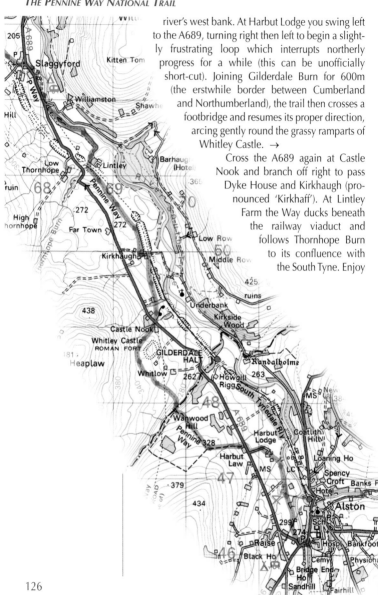

river's west bank. At Harbut Lodge you swing left to the A689, turning right then left to begin a slightly frustrating loop which interrupts northerly progress for a while (this can be unofficially short-cut). Joining Gilderdale Burn for 600m (the erstwhile border between Cumberland and Northumberland), the trail then crosses a footbridge and resumes its proper direction, arcing gently round the grassy ramparts of Whitley Castle. →

Cross the A689 again at Castle Nook and branch off right to pass Dyke House and Kirkhaugh (pronounced 'Kirkhaff'). At Lintley Farm the Way ducks beneath the railway viaduct and follows Thornhope Burn to its confluence with the South Tyne. Enjoy

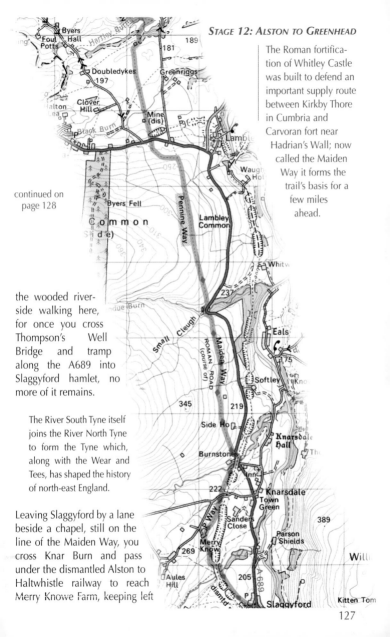

The Roman fortification of Whitley Castle was built to defend an important supply route between Kirkby Thore in Cumbria and Carvoran fort near Hadrian's Wall; now called the Maiden Way it forms the trail's basis for a few miles ahead.

continued on page 128

the wooded riverside walking here, for once you cross Thompson's Well Bridge and tramp along the A689 into Slaggyford hamlet, no more of it remains.

The River South Tyne itself joins the River North Tyne to form the Tyne which, along with the Wear and Tees, has shaped the history of north-east England.

Leaving Slaggyford by a lane beside a chapel, still on the line of the Maiden Way, you cross Knar Burn and pass under the dismantled Alston to Haltwhistle railway to reach Merry Knowe Farm, keeping left

127

of the buildings. More field walking ensues to Burnstones Farm, crossing a country lane to Knarsdale and the Thinhope Burn on the way.

From Burnstones the trail rises along the lower edge of Glendue Fell, straight and direct as a Roman roadway should be. Glendue Burn is crossed next to the A689 road hairpin, whereafter you maintain satisfying northerly progress over the heather-clad slopes of Lambley Common, a grouse shooting moor.

For the very last time the A689 is crossed near Lambley village in an area of old colliery and mine workings where even the vegetation seems more than usually sour. Beyond Black Burn the trail runs on over neglected, dreary pasture to High House ruin but improves as it crosses Hartley Burn. Pastureland leads you past Batey Shield Farm and over Kellah Burn at a country road. Turn left up to Greenriggs cottage, passing it to the left (west) and continue over the low,

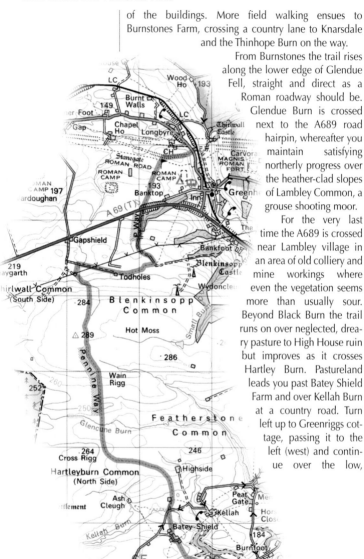

rather desolate moors of Round Hill and Wain Rigg. Passing about 150m east of Blade Hill's trig pillar at a mere 948ft (289m) above sea level, the Way drops to Gap Shields and for the first time you have a really clear view of the Whin Sill crags upon which Hadrian's Wall is built. Veering sharp right along a track past old colliery shafts then left to the busy A69 might even put a spring back into your step!

Although tantalisingly close (only ½ mile (1km) to the east), Greenhead is reached more pleasingly, and certainly more safely, by keeping to the onward Pennine Way which crosses the road, climbs the bank opposite and proceeds over fields and a golf course to arrive at the Vallum; this is followed east to the B6318 with Greenhead lying just along to your right.

The Vallum, first of the Roman structures to be met, is a wide ditch which accompanies the Wall throughout its length and denoted the southern perimeter of the linear military zone.

At Greenhead, situated in the Carlisle-Newcastle gap, the North Pennines end. It is a modest village but one at which accommodation and supplies may be obtained, as well as bus and rail transport and perhaps a drink in the Greenhead Hotel.

STAGE 13
Greenhead to Housesteads Fort

In the sense that you will not be staying overnight at Housesteads (a marvellously preserved Roman fort owned by the National Trust and situated about ½ mile (1km) off-route), this stage is an artificial one logistically. However, Hadrian's Wall forms such a distinctive section of trail that it is best described on its own. There are several accommodation places just south of the Wall, including a youth hostel, suggesting a short day with plenty of time allowed to savour this most famous of all Britain's Roman monuments. Alternatively, accommodation could be booked in one of the farms on the trail some distance ahead. Only the strongest walkers among us will aim to reach Bellingham, still 13½ miles (22km) beyond the Wall. Although the Wall captures the imagination and provides a continual focus of interest, the walking itself is moderately strenuous in places as you climb and drop above the steep crags of the Whin Sill, exposed to wind and weather.

The Pennine Way resumes at Thirlwall Castle north of Greenhead, its romantic, crumbling ruin overlooking tree-fringed Tipalt Burn. ←

This 14th-century peel tower was built using mainly Roman stones – one reason why the Wall has vanished here almost without trace.

Crossing Tipalt Burn and continuing on a track through trees, the Way rises beside the defensive ditch and enters the Northumberland

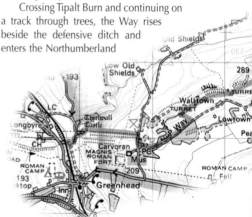

Distance:	12 miles (19km)
Main Ascents:	Numerous ups and downs culminating in the highest point at Winshields Crag – 1132ft (345m)
Refreshments: (on/near route)	Pubs, shops and services at Haltwhistle; seasonal snack bar at Cawfields car park; Twice Brewed Inn; Milecastle Inn near Cawfields
Public transport:	Buses from Twice Brewed to Carlisle and Newcastle; summer season buses between Hexham and the main Wall sites; trains from Haltwhistle to Carlisle and Newcastle
Accommodation:	B&Bs at Haltwhistle and Twice Brewed; youth hostel at Once Brewed; camping at Winshields Farm
Maps:	OS Landranger Sheet 86, OS Explorer Sheet 43

National Park. Turning right along a lane ahead brings you to the site of Carvoran fort, now a Roman Army Museum well worth taking in if time allows. Follow the eastbound stony lane opposite at Walltown and beyond Walltown Quarry bear left uphill to reach Walltown Crags (or the Nine Nicks of Thirlwall) near Turret 45a. Here at last Hadrian's Wall is joined and will accompany you for the next few miles, so a little background information may be useful.

continued on page 132

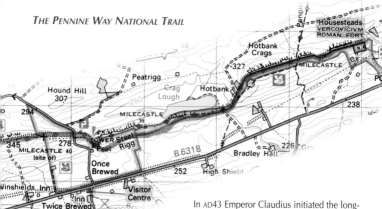

In AD43 Emperor Claudius initiated the long-expected invasion of Britain which would leave an indelible mark upon the country's history. The Roman army, 50,000 strong, was the largest in the world and although Iron Age Britons were resourceful and skilled in many ways (in the south at least), they were no match for the disciplined Romans who advanced speedily north and west. Despite steady progress, it was not until after AD80 that the Caledonian tribes of northern Britain were finally defeated. However, the Highlands proved difficult and unprofitable so eventually troops were withdrawn.

In AD122, already Emperor for five years, Hadrian visited Britain and ordered a great defensive wall to be built against the still troublesome northern barbarians. It would run 76 miles (122km) from Wallsend on the Tyne to Bowness-on-Solway and would be constructed by professional legionary craftsmen. There would be guard posts (milecastles), watch towers (turrets) and forts at regular intervals. As well as a forward defensive ditch, a second – the Vallum – was dug behind the Wall to secure the military zone.

By around AD130 the Wall was completed, though only of turf to begin with in the western sector. The building of the Antonine Wall 85 miles (137km) further north in AD142 failed to hold territory there and in the face of continuing hostility by marauding tribesmen Hadrian's Wall once again became the official frontier of Roman Britain. It would remain thus for the next 200 years.

A stout and solid stretch of Hadrian's Wall running across Cawfield Crags (Photograph by Paddy Dillon)

Today much of the original structure (probably some 15ft (5m) high) is lost beneath the streets of Newcastle and the 18th-century military road. Over the centuries, stone has also been appropriated for building and repairing farms. Nevertheless, what does remain still provides us with a vivid evocation of that momentous era in Britain's development. Pennine wayfarers are fortunate to witness the best preserved section of Wall, often shoulder-high and snaking ahead over undulations in the ground.

In 1995 plans for a new National Trail along Hadrian's Wall were initiated, due to open in May 2003. As a matter of plain common sense walkers should respect the value of this unique antiquity by keeping to the flanking paths: walking on the walltop itself, however tempting, causes structural damage and is to be discouraged at all times.

From Walltown Crags the onward trail dips at Milecastle 44 and follows a re-aligned routing past Cockmount Farm and the fragmentary remains of Aesica fort. Beyond the road you pass Cawfields car park and picnic area by the old quarry lake. A climb past Milecastle 42 surmounts rugged Cawfield Crags followed by a descent to another lane at Shield on the Wall.

Pennine wayfarers follow the roller-coaster course of Hadrian's Wall (Photograph by Paddy Dillon)

In clear air views are extensive, embracing Cross Fell, the Cheviots, the Solway Firth and the North Sea. Hardy black Galloway cattle and Blackface or Swaledale sheep punctuate a landscape of hilly pasture, field patchworks and the dark edges of forestry. Whatever the weather, this is hillwalking at its most atmospheric.

Throughout the walk along here there is a succession of ups and downs, some quite steep, as you follow the undulating crest of the Whin Sill. Ice and meltwater exploited weaknesses in the ridge during two-million years of ice ages, forming the gaps we find today. This is the self-same band of dolerite, or basalt, that created the Tees waterfalls and High Cup. Gentler slopes of pasture-land to the south swell to an escarpment of precipitous crags – precisely the kind of natural high ground that an army needed to repel attack from the north.

Rising past Milecastle 41 the trail reaches the trig pillar at 1132ft (345m) atop heathery Winshields Crag, highest summit on the entire Roman Wall. ←

An easy descent brings you to Peel Gap and the National Park's Steel Rigg car park. Just to the south pub, youth hostel and, a little further east, the Vindolanda Museum can be found. There is a Northumberland National Park Visitor Centre at Once Brewed. The ascent to Peel Crags is so steep that steps have been installed. There follows a sharp drop to pass Milecastle 39 (Castle Nick) then a traverse above the steely waters of Crag Lough; below the exposed edge are Highshields Crags containing some rock-climbing routes. Descending through mixed woodland to Milking Gap, the trail continues east past Hotbank Farm near the site of Milecastle 38 before rising over Hotbank Crags (1074ft (327m)) with panoramas over the nearby loughs.

Soon the Way reaches Rapishaw Gap where it bids farewell to the Wall and heads north towards Wark Forest. However, unless very pressed for time a detour to Housesteads fort is strongly recommended. It is found by simply continuing ahead past Milecastle 37 – a distance of just over ½ mile (1km) each way out and back.

> Housesteads (Verovicium) is owned by the National Trust and ranks as one of the finest Roman hilltop fort remains in Britain. It is therefore well visited. The site is immensely impressive (despite the incongruous, though functional, surfaced pathways). Sufficient masonry exists for one's imagination to visualise how the complex would have once looked, though for the full picture it is advisable to see the Visitor Centre displays nearby to the south.

OTHER CONNECTING TRAILS

Hadrian's Wall Path: The 75 mile (120km) waymarked trail extends from the Cumbrian coast to Newcastle-upon-Tyne, closely following the Wall throughout its length using a combination of public footpaths, tracks and country lanes.
Start: Wallsend, Tyne and Wear (NZ 304660)
Finish: Bowness-on-Solway, Cumbria (NY 225628)
OS Landranger Sheets: 85, 86, 87, 88

STAGE 14
Hadrian's Wall (Rapishaw Gap)
to Bellingham

A combination of low moorland, forestry and farmland characterises this section of trail. Only the eastern fringes of the great Border forests are penetrated by the Pennine Way and perhaps that is just as well: tramping along forestry roads devoid of views and wayside interest is anathema to most walkers. Only in the roughest of weather is the shelter provided by the densely planted trees a welcome feature. With the Roman Wall now behind you there may be a growing awareness that the end is in sight; but it is not all downhill yet!

At Rapishaw Gap the trail strikes off north over rough grass and heather to cross Jenkins Burn between Broomlee and Greenlee loughs.

The stretches of open water of Jenkins Burn and Bromlee and Greenlee loughs are the remnants of glacial meltwater from the end of the last Ice Age some 12,000 years ago. Plant growth is slowly encroaching and it seems likely that the loughs will one day become mere marshy depressions. In the meantime they support

Distance:	13½ miles (22km)
Main Ascents:	Esp Mill to Ealingham Rigg – 328ft (100m)
Refreshments: (on/near route)	Possible seasonal refreshments at Horneystead Farm; all shops and services at Bellingham
Public transport:	Buses from Bellingham to Hexham (trains to Newcastle)
Accommodation:	B&Bs at Hetherington, Horneystead Farm, Low Stead and Bellingham; youth hostel at Bellingham; camping and bunkhouse at Horneystead Farm and Shitlington Cragg Farm, camping at Bellingham
Maps:	OS Landranger Sheets 86 and 80, OS Explorer Sheet 42

continued on page 138

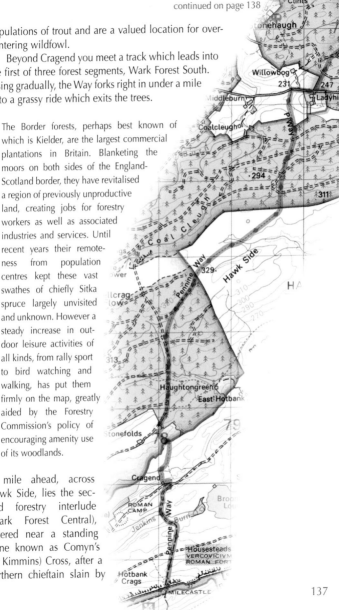

populations of trout and are a valued location for over-wintering wildfowl.

Beyond Cragend you meet a track which leads into the first of three forest segments, Wark Forest South. Rising gradually, the Way forks right in under a mile onto a grassy ride which exits the trees.

The Border forests, perhaps best known of which is Kielder, are the largest commercial plantations in Britain. Blanketing the moors on both sides of the England-Scotland border, they have revitalised a region of previously unproductive land, creating jobs for forestry workers as well as associated industries and services. Until recent years their remoteness from population centres kept these vast swathes of chiefly Sitka spruce largely unvisited and unknown. However a steady increase in outdoor leisure activities of all kinds, from rally sport to bird watching and walking, has put them firmly on the map, greatly aided by the Forestry Commission's policy of encouraging amenity use of its woodlands.

A mile ahead, across Hawk Side, lies the second forestry interlude (Wark Forest Central), entered near a standing stone known as Comyn's (or Kimmins) Cross, after a northern chieftain slain by

137

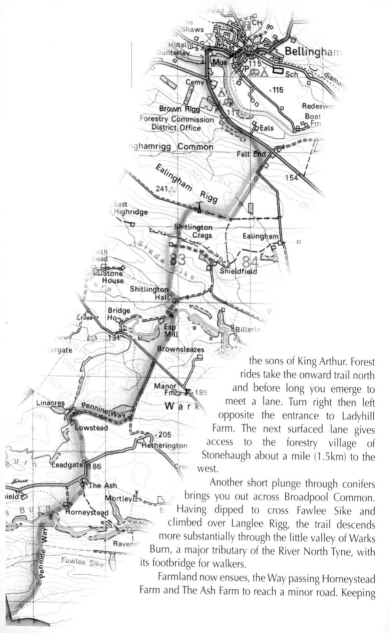

the sons of King Arthur. Forest rides take the onward trail north and before long you emerge to meet a lane. Turn right then left opposite the entrance to Ladyhill Farm. The next surfaced lane gives access to the forestry village of Stonehaugh about a mile (1.5km) to the west.

Another short plunge through conifers brings you out across Broadpool Common. Having dipped to cross Fawlee Sike and climbed over Langlee Rigg, the trail descends more substantially through the little valley of Warks Burn, a major tributary of the River North Tyne, with its footbridge for walkers.

Farmland now ensues, the Way passing Horneystead Farm and The Ash Farm to reach a minor road. Keeping north past Leadgate Farm leads to Lowstead, a picturesque complex of buildings built around a former 16th-century fortified farmhouse. Here the trail jinks east past the entrance to modern Linacres and at the access road's junction ahead turns left.

A kilometre along the road (now heading north-north-east), carry straight on into a field path, bearing left to cross the tree-fringed Houxty Burn footbridge then immediately right to cross a tributary footbridge. An access road leads up past Shitlington Hall Farm and an uphill field path takes you on to Shitlington Cragg Farm and a line of low crags bearing the same name!

Aiming now just west of a radio mast, the Way meets a cart track on Ealingham Rigg (791ft (241m)) and follows it east until directed by a waymark sign left over damp moorland to the corner of a minor lane. A left fork over pasture and you are walking beside the B6320 Wark road for the stage's last mile into Bellingham (pronounced 'Bellinjam').

Countryside flanking the North Tyne's delightful valley represents the final pastoral landscape on the trek north until the descent is made from the Cheviots. Bellingham, a lively market town with all shops, services and accommodation, provides Pennine wayfarers with a chance to re-stock supplies and plan the route's push onward to Kirk Yetholm, now only 45 miles (72km) distant.

STAGE 15
Bellingham to Byrness

Hillside pastures give way to moorland of heather, marsh and rough grass as the trail leaves Bellingham on its final approach to the Cheviot Hills. It is not a stage of distinction, more a means to an end, and includes a longish tramp through the eastern section of Redesdale Forest. However, in all but the worst weather there is an uplifting sense of spaciousness to begin with as views extend forward to the Cheviots. Reaching the tiny community of Byrness on the River Rede is guaranteed to generate excitement and anticipation at the prospect of completing the Pennine Way.

From Bellingham take the West Woodburn road which dips to cross Hareshaw Burn, and fork left up the lane past the youth hostel. Where this swings sharp right, carry straight on, passing through Blakelaw farmyard and aiming uphill over pasture towards a skyline conifer plantation. Once there you pass through a gate to cross heather and bracken clad moorland, entering the Northumberland National Park at the head of Conheath Burn.

Down to the west in its wooded glen, Hareshaw Lin waterfall cascades prettily over rocky ledges. Unfortunately there is no access from the Pennine Way,

Distance:	15½ miles (25km)
Main Ascents:	Bellingham to Padon Hill – 804ft (245m)
Refreshments: (on/near route)	Cafe and hotel at Byrness
Public transport:	Buses from Byrness to Newcastle and Edinburgh
Accommodation:	B&Bs, youth hostel, bunkhouse and camping at Byrness
Maps:	OS Landranger Sheet 80, OS Explorer Sheet 42

continued on
page 142

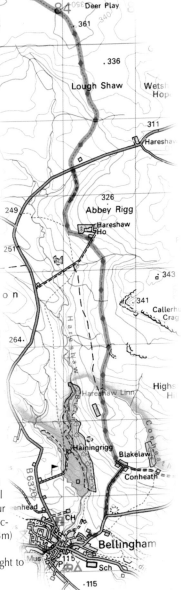

the only right-of-way
being a path from
Bellingham which, nevertheless, is well worth exploring.

Keeping to the higher ground in
preference to the left-hand fork, the
trail continues over two feeder streams
to Hareshaw House Farm. The broad
onward track, once a narrow gauge colliery railway line that closed in the 1950s
after two centuries of operation, takes
you to the B6320 Bellingham/
Otterburn road. Opposite there begins
a steady haul up over heathery Lough
Shaw and Deer Play (1184ft (361m)),
with increasingly wide views to distant
moorland horizons, including the
Padon Hill monument. Ahead the Way
has been realigned to follow the more
direct route to Whitley Pike on Lord's
Shaw (1168ft (356m)) and there are flagstones on the short stretch parallel to a
fence leading down to the unenclosed
Troughend/Gibshiel road.

> In its early days the Pennine Way turned
> left along the tarmac and into Redesdale
> Forest via Gibshiel, but no-one enjoys
> road walking if there is an alternative. The
> present alignment over Padon Hill and
> Brownrigg Head is far preferable.

Still beside a fence, the Way now rises
across the west shoulder of Padon Hill
whose 1243ft (379m) summit over to your
right is crowned by a very large and distinctive 'pepperbox' monument some 15ft (3m)
high.

The monument on Padon Hill is thought to

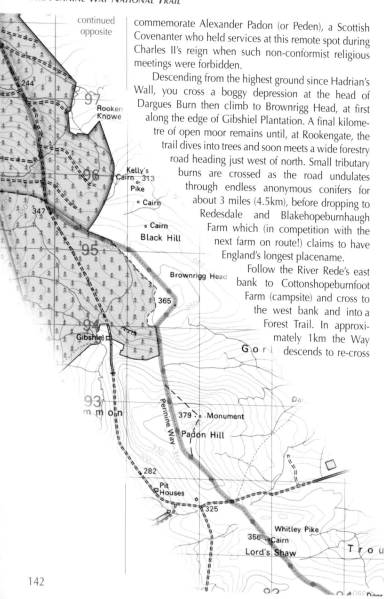

commemorate Alexander Padon (or Peden), a Scottish Covenanter who held services at this remote spot during Charles II's reign when such non-conformist religious meetings were forbidden.

Descending from the highest ground since Hadrian's Wall, you cross a boggy depression at the head of Dargues Burn then climb to Brownrigg Head, at first along the edge of Gibshiel Plantation. A final kilometre of open moor remains until, at Rookengate, the trail dives into trees and soon meets a wide forestry road heading just west of north. Small tributary burns are crossed as the road undulates through endless anonymous conifers for about 3 miles (4.5km), before dropping to Redesdale and Blakehopeburnhaugh Farm which (in competition with the next farm on route!) claims to have England's longest placename.

Follow the River Rede's east bank to Cottonshopeburnfoot Farm (campsite) and cross to the west bank and into a Forest Trail. In approximately 1km the Way descends to re-cross the river and rises to meet the A68 Newcastle-Edinburgh road at Byrness.

With a youth hostel, bed and breakfast places, a hotel, campsite and roadside cafe, Byrness despite its diminutive size, takes on considerable significance for northbound Pennine wayfarers. It is positively the last enclave of civilised amenities before the climactic 28 mile (45km) trek across the Cheviot tops. Now is the time to check your gear (and perhaps your blisters!), to obtain a weather forecast and to stock up with sufficient food and drink (including emergency rations) to last until Kirk

Yetholm. (The only exception being those having booked an overnight stop midway which involves a lengthy descent from the Cheviot ridge and, of course, a reascent the following morning.)

Byrness itself was originally established to accommodate construction workers building the nearby Catcleugh Reservoir. It was later adopted as a Forestry Commission village to enable the planting and subsequent management of Redesdale Forest, witness the distinctive terrace of forestry dwellings.

STAGE 16
Byrness to Kirk Yetholm

If this stage is tackled in one day – and it often is – a good deal of effort is involved. As always when accommodation is in short supply, lightweight campers enjoy a distinct advantage, despite having to carry extra gear: there are several favoured spots for an overnight camp, among them Chew Green and the Windy Gyle area. The only accommodation other than a tent are B&Bs in the flanking valleys, namely Greenhill (2½miles (4km) north-north-west from Lamb Hill); and Uswayford (1½ miles (2.5km) south-east of the ridge between Windy Gyle and King's Seat). Check with the local tourist office as to B&B availability before tackling this section.

Throughout the stage water is hard to find, unless you descend into the upper reaches of a burn. Bear in mind that the map cannot guarantee there will be running water or that it will be drinkable; in mist, locating such possible sources of water may be problematic.

Distance:	28 miles (45km)
Main Ascents:	Byrness to Byrness Hill – 636ft (194m); several minor climbs averaging 100ft (30m) over subsidiary tops on the Cheviot ridge; Butt Roads to Cairn Hill west top – 732ft (223m); Cairn Hill west top to The Cheviot – 236ft (72m)
Refreshments: (on/near route)	none
Public transport:	Buses from Town Yetholm to Jedburgh (for Newcastle) and Kelso/Berwick-upon-Tweed (for East Coast trains)
Accommodation:	Very limited B&Bs off route at Greenhill (to the west) and Uswayford (to the east); B&Bs at Kirk Yetholm and Town Yetholm; youth hostel and camping at Kirk Yetholm
Maps:	OS Landranger Sheets 80 and 74, OS Explorer Sheet 16

continued on page 146

Once you have climbed away from Redesdale Forest the trail passes Chew Green Roman camp and meets the Scotland/England border. Happily for navigation in mist, the border is defined, more or less, by a fence, although here and there the Pennine Way cuts off corners. The route itself follows a convoluted ridge that marks the watershed between the River Coquet to the east and Kale Water to the west. The watershed's many lateral ridges and side valleys covering a very extensive area make for confusion when position-finding is attempted, though the trail is considerably easier to follow since the installation of flagstones on stretches where there was once boot-sucking bog. Even so, this extended hillwalk is a serious undertaking, all the more so should weather conditions be hostile. There is very little shelter without making a lengthy deviation from the route. All this said, in reasonable weather the high level crossing is greatly rewarding, both for its solitude and wide open spaces and for the sense of achievement it brings when completed.

Making an early start, or delaying your departure in particularly poor weather, can both contribute in their different ways to a successful outcome. However, the sheer momentum to reach Kirk Yetholm come what may is hard to resist. The common sense advice must be: know your limitations and plan accordingly.

From about 100m along the A68 north-west of the Byrness Hotel the onward trail forks right. When you reach Byrness Cottage you are faced with a steep and quite protracted climb on a grassy forest ride which eventually brings you out above the trees on Byrness Hill. Passing Saughy Crag, one of several hilltop outcrops hereabouts, the path leads on north to Houx Hill above Windy Crag. Accompanied by a fence the Way continues over Ravens Knowe (1729ft (527m)) to Ogre Hill and the border fence itself which is met at the northernmost extremity of Redesdale Forest. Crossing the fence takes you into Scottish territory for the first time, whereupon you veer east and descend back into

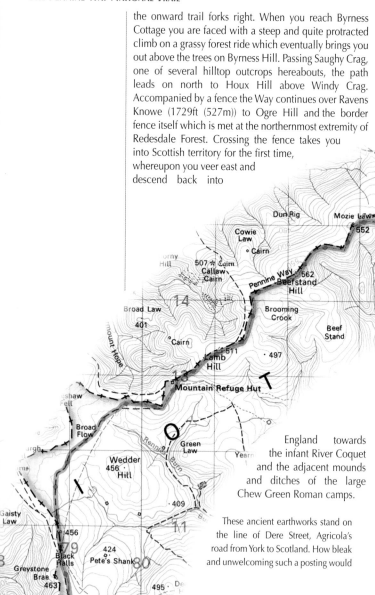

England towards the infant River Coquet and the adjacent mounds and ditches of the large Chew Green Roman camps.

These ancient earthworks stand on the line of Dere Street, Agricola's road from York to Scotland. How bleak and unwelcoming such a posting would

continued on
page 148

White Knowe
Settlement

King's Seat
Cairn

·531

The Bank

·418

Butt Roads

Cairn

Cairn

Cairn

520

ossy
_aw

Windy Rig

561

Cairn

Russell's Cairn

·619

Cairn

Windy Gyle

H

Little
·495

*The trail through
Redesdale Forest*

have seemed to those Romans
legionnaires garrisoned here, compared with their
Mediterranean homeland. The region's military
associations persist, for a great swathe of hills to
the east and south are owned by the Ministry of
Defence, based on their Otterburn camp. The
sound of firing on the ranges often assails the ears
of passing Pennine wayfarers! There is a small car
park at the end of the tortuous tarmac road which
shadows the River Coquet all the way up into
these hills from Alwinton in Coquetdale; it is a
safe escape route if one is needed.

Passing round to the east of the encampments,
the trail crosses the top of Chew Sike, still for
the time being on the line of Dere Street. It
enters Scotland again at the border fence not
far from Brownhart Law but quickly reverts
back to the English side. At a gate shortly

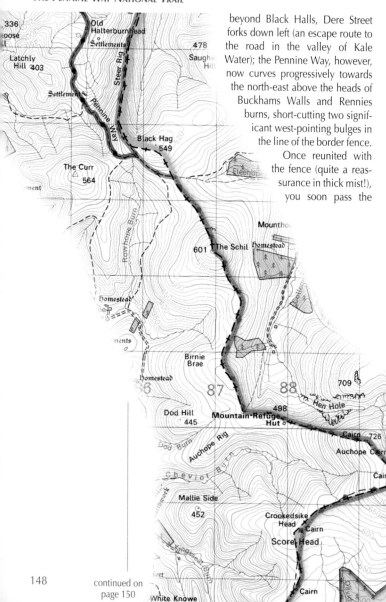

beyond Black Halls, Dere Street forks down left (an escape route to the road in the valley of Kale Water); the Pennine Way, however, now curves progressively towards the north-east above the heads of Buckhams Walls and Rennies burns, short-cutting two significant west-pointing bulges in the line of the border fence.

Once reunited with the fence (quite a reassurance in thick mist!), you soon pass the

continued on page 150

timber refuge hut (a useful emergency or bad weather shelter) situated to the south-west of Lamb Hill. In close proximity to the fence from now on, if not actually beside it, the trail climbs over Lamb Hill (1676ft (511m)) then over Beefstand Hill (1844ft (562m)) and over Mozie Law (1811ft (552m)), with exciting views ahead to Windy Gyle and the brooding bulk of The Cheviot. The next descent brings you to a well-known cross-border drove road called The Street running north-west over the range from upper Coquetdale to Calroust and providing another possible escape route off these tops.

Pennine Wayfarers march through the broad and bleak Cheviot Hills (Photograph by Paddy Dillon)

The Way continues without difficulty to Russell's Cairn on Windy Gyle (2031ft (619m)), roughly the stage's halfway point and the highest summit on the ridge so far. There are paths on both sides of the border fence approaching the cairn but the onward trail reverts to the English side. Just over a mile ahead, another ancient thoroughfare – Clennell Street – crosses the route at Border Gate. (A possible camping spot. Down to the south-east stands Uswayford Farm offering B&B and camping. In either direction, Clennell Street provides the last chance to leave the ridge before The Cheviot.)

King's Seat is the next summit in line, followed by Score Head then a more sustained pull up to the west top of Cairn Hill. Here at 2438ft (743m) the border fence makes an abrupt turn from east-north-east to north-west.

The 1.4 miles (2.25km) each way to claim The Cheviot summit itself may or may not appeal to you. Much will depend on the time of day, the weather and levels of fatigue. For some, bagging the summit represents the essential culmination of the Cheviot stage, a rousing finale to the whole Pennine Way. For others, the detour is seen as an unnecessary appendage to an already testing walk, an obstacle to reaching the real goal of Kirk Yetholm. If you decide to make the diversion, flagstones have taken the sting out of the previously squelchy journey, just as they have on other stretches of trail. Although reaching 2674ft (815m), The Cheviot, it must be said, is not the most uplifting of tops, rather a featureless plateau whose views are limited by its very expansiveness. Any satisfaction gained will derive from the knowledge that this is the highest ground in the region.

*Looking west from
Cairn Hill west top near
Cheviot summit*

Having retraced steps to the corner in the border fence, or simply continuing on from there, you now begin the final leg of the trek. At first soggy terrain persists but from Auchope Cairn (2382ft (726m)) the going is not only downhill but over good firm grass. A National Park shelter provides welcome respite in poor weather and shortly after, where the border fence makes a sharp turn above the Red Cribs landslip, there is a wonderful view up the valley of College Burn to the cliffs of Hen Hole.

With a couple of minor undulations the trail reaches The Schil (1972ft (601m)), shapeliest of the Cheviot summits, crowned by a rocky tor and ringed by scree. Descending by fence and wall you climb a stile at the saddle before Black Hag to pass into Scotland.

A dilemma now confronts you. The Way proper continues north over Steerrig Knowe and White Law – a not inconsiderable climb coming as it usually does at the day's end. As a clear track it then heads north-west from the border on Stob Rig, crosses the Halter Burn and joins the tarmac road for the last mile or so to Kirk Yetholm. Alternatively, a 'bad weather' route turns its back on the heights by threading down past Latchly Hill and the ruins of Old Halterburnhead to Burnhead Farm which it passes just to the east of the buildings. A surfaced lane then steers you with no further complications past Halterburn Farm, joining the main route and rising over the shoulder of Staerough Hill to arrive at journey's end.

This is a moment to savour! Whether you have completed the Pennine Way in sections or in one continuous trek,

There could hardly be a more pleasant place at which to end than Kirk Yetholm, a quiet border village of neat houses set round a green. It is customary to have a celebratory drink (or three!) in the Border Hotel before planning a return to 'normality' which usually involves catching a bus to Kelso from neighbouring Town Yetholm. One thing is certain: the Pennine Way will have left an indelible mark upon your life.

you have every reason for self-congratulation. Few walkers enjoy a trouble-free journey; indeed, only a fraction of those setting out actually finish. But on any long-distance trail, overcoming setbacks and facing adversity are as much part of the experience as the walking itself, the scenery, friends made along the way. ←

OTHER CONNECTING TRAILS

Three Peaks of Cheviot Challenge Walk: A 30 mile (48km) tough, high-level walk which takes in The Schil, Windy Gyle and Hedgehope Hill. As an official challenge the walk is undertaken between April and September.

Start and Finish: Hawsen Burn, Northumbria (NT 954225)

OS Landranger Sheets: 74, 75, 80

Other Cicerone Press Guides for routes mentioned in this Guide

The Alternative Pennine Way, Denis Brook and Phil Hinchliffe

The Dales Way, Terry Marsh

The Teesdale Way, Martin Collins

A Northern Coast to Coast, Terry Marsh

The Alternative Coast to Coast, Denis Brook and Phil Hinchliffe

Hadrian's Wall Vol. I: The Wall Walk, Mark Richards

also:

Laughs along the Pennine Way, Pete Bogg

APPENDIX A:
Regional Tourist Boards and Tourist Information Centres on or nearest to the Pennine Way

Heart of England Tourist Board
Woodside
Larkhill Road
Worcesteshire
WR5 2EZ
Tel: (01905) 763 436

Yorkshire and Humberside Tourist Board
312 Tadcaster Road
York YO2 2HF
Tel: (01904) 707961

Cumbria Tourist Board
Ashleigh
Holly Road
Windermere
Cumbria LA23 2AQ
Tel: (015394) 44041

Northumbria Tourist Board
Aykley Heads
Durham DH1 5UX
Tel: (0191) 384 6905

Scottish Tourist Board
19 Cockspur Street
London SW1Y 5BL
Tel: (0845) 2255 121

Edale
National Park Visitor Centre
Fieldhead
Edale
Derbyshire
Tel: (01433) 670207

Glossop
Derbyshire
Tel: (01457) 855920

Hebden Bridge
West Yorkshire
Tel: (01422) 843831

Haworth
West Yorkshire
Tel: (01535) 642329

Skipton
North Yorkshire
Tel: (01756) 792809

Settle
North Yorkshire
Tel: (01729) 825192

Horton-in-Ribblesdale
North Yorkshire
Pen-y-Ghent Cafe
Tel: (01729) 860333

Yorkshire Dales National Park Centre
Hawes
North Yorkshire
Tel: (01969) 667450

Middleton-in-Teesdale
Tel: (01642) 243425

Appleby-in-Westmorland
Cumbria
Tel: (01768) 351177

Alston
Cumbria
Tel: (01434) 3812244

Haltwhistle
Northumbria
Tel: (01434) 322002

Once Brewed Visitor Centre
Military Road

Bardon Mill
Northumbria
Tel: (01434) 344396

Hexham
Northumbria
Tel: (01434) 652220

Bellingham
Northumbria
Tel: (01434) 220616

Kelso
Borders Region
Tel: (01573) 223464

APPENDIX B:
Useful Addresses

Pennine Way National Trail
Steven Westwood
Pennine Way National Trail Officer
The Countryside Agency
4th Floor, Victoria Wharf
No 4 The Embankment
Leeds LS1 4BA
Tel: (0113) 246 9222
Fax: (0113) 246 0353

Pennine Way Association
John Needham
23 Woodland Crescent
Hilton Park
Manchester M25 9WQ

Camping and Caravanning Club
Greenfields House
Westwood Way
Coventry
West Midlands CV4 8JH
Tel: (024) 7669 4995

Countryside Agency
John Dower House
Crescent Place
Cheltenham
Glos GL50 3RA
Tel: (01242) 521381

English Heritage
Customer Services Department
PO Box 569
Swindon
SN2 2YP
Tel: (0870) 333 1181

Forestry Commission
231 Corstorphine Road
Edinburgh EH12 7AT
Tel: (0131) 334 0303

Long Distance Walkers Association
Membership Secretary
63 Yockley Close
Camberley
Surrey GU15 1QQ

National Trust
36 Queen Anne's Gate
London SW1H 9AS
Tel: (0870) 609 5380

Ordnance Survey
Romsey Road
Maybush
Southampton SO9 4DH
Tel: (0845) 605 0 505

Ramblers' Association
2nd Floor Camelford House
87–90 Albert Embankment
London SE1 7TW
Tel: (020) 7339 8500

Youth Hostels Association
Trevelyan House
Dimple Road
Matlock
Derbyshire DE4 3YH
Tel: (0870) 8708808

Youth Hostels Association
Booking Bureau
PO Box 6028
Matlock
Derbyshire DE4 3XB
Tel: (0870) 2412314
Fax: (01629) 592627

LISTING OF CICERONE GUIDES

Cicerone's mission is to inform and inspire by
providing the best guides to exploring the world

Since its foundation over 30 years ago, Cicerone has specialised in
publishing guidebooks and has built a reputation for quality and reliability.
It now publishes nearly 300 guides to the major destinations for outdoor
enthusiasts, including Europe, UK and the rest of the world.

Written by leading and committed specialists, Cicerone guides are
recognised as the most authoritative. They are full of information, maps and
illustrations so that the user can plan and complete a successful and safe
trip or expedition – be it a long face climb, a walk over Lakeland fells, an
alpine traverse, a Himalayan trek or a ramble in the countryside.

With a thorough introduction to assist planning, clear diagrams, maps and
colour photographs to illustrate the terrain and route, and accurate and
detailed text, Cicerone guides are designed for ease of use and access to
the information.

If the facts on the ground change, or there is any aspect of a guide that you
think we can improve, we are always delighted to hear from you.

Cicerone Press
2 Police Square Milnthorpe Cumbria LA7 7PY
Tel:01539 562 069   Fax:01539 563 417
e-mail:info@cicerone.co.uk   web:www.cicerone.co.uk

CICERONE